100 BEST IDEAS FOR Primary Science

Written by
Beverly Hartman

Illustrated by Becky J. Radtke

Teaching & Learning Company

1204 Buchanan St., P.O. Box 10
Carthage, IL 62321

This book belongs to

_____

To the memory of my father
Herbert A. Hirschman
(1916-1992)

This book was developed for the Teaching & Learning Company
by The Good Neighbor Press, Inc., Grand Junction, CO.

Cover illustration by Nancee McClure

Copyright © 1994, Teaching & Learning Company

ISBN No. 1-57310-002-1

Printing No. 9876

Teaching & Learning Company
1204 Buchanan St., P.O. Box 10
Carthage, IL 62321

Table of Contents

Dear Teacher,

Did you know that science-based questions are those most asked by the young child? As an early childhood educator you can ride the coattails of this marvelous, built-in curiosity and lead your students to some fun and fascinating learning experiences. The hands-on activities in this book will help build a firm foundation of skills and thinking processes that will help lead to scientific literacy in your students. Although that might sound rather lofty, the amazing progress we see in our world today is based in science. We find children coming to us with science awareness and knowledge that make science education a natural in today's classroom. Please read through this section before embarking on your learning journey. The "why" and "how" of the activities are explained and will help you with the presentation of all your science activities.

Science Process Skills

Science sometimes seems unapproachable because of its complicated vocabulary. The introduction of science process vocabulary at the exact time a certain skill is being used will bring immediate life to unfamiliar terminology. This book targets eight such skills and identifies those used in each activity.

Let your students know that they are. . .

comparing and contrasting when they look for things that are different or similar during a science activity. *Compare:* What parts do all animals have that are alike? *Contrast:* What differences can you see between trees in the summer and trees in the winter?

describing when they use their senses to verbally explain what can be learned about an object or happening. *Example:* What do you hear, feel and see when you breathe in?

experimenting when they test things in the environment to learn answers to a scientific inquiry. *Example:* What happens when you let salt water sit in the open air for along time?

identifying when they recognize familiar things in nature or a pattern of behavior in nature. *Example:* Which cloud will make it rain?

measuring when they use observation or the tools of science to obtain information. *Example:* How much do you weigh?

observing when they use their senses to obtain information. *Example:* What did the mouse do when he saw you?

predicting outcomes when they use prior knowledge or experience to predict what will happen in the future. *Example:* What will happen if we put liquid water in the freezer?

recording data when they in some way preserve their measurements and observations. *Example:* Write down how many ladybugs you found on the shrub.

Scientific Method

There are as many versions of the scientific method as there are books to describe it! For the young child, the scientific method is best presented as an orderly way of examining the world of science. The activities in this book are presented in a manner that will establish an order of events. The steps used are …

Experimenting/Observing: This step is the actual hands-on component of each activity. The student will be testing and then observing the results of his testing.

Thinking: This step is the analyzing and synthesizing of information that the child has learned through experimentation and observation.

Explaining: Forming conclusions as a result of the above steps. Most children will form appropriate conclusions. If not, this is where the teacher can gently lead children's thinking to a conclusion.

Science Teaching Methods

Because of the importance of scientific literacy for everyone in today's world, much reflective thought is being given to science education in K-12. The overwhelming conclusion seems to be that children can reach understanding and long-term retention of that understanding when they are able to experience science themselves. When their hands (and eyes, and noses) are involved, their minds are fully engaged in learning. This book is based on that certainty. In addition to this method, two others have been included in the activities in this book:

Engage Activities: These are designed to get children focused on that specific area of science included in the activity. It should "boot up" everything that children already know and prepare them to add new knowledge. It should also serve as an effort to get them interested and excited about what is going to happen!

Expanded Activities: When your students are really excited about an activity and want to carry it further, this section contains some suggestions for doing so. Some of the activities will build upon each other—from one page to the next. These are also expansions.

Also included are **Science Notes** for each activity. If you are like most of us, you will feel more comfortable about presenting activities when you know a bit more than your students. It is the rare science teacher who doesn't review (and even relearn) the science material being presented. These science notes are included for your review, interest, curiosity and understanding of the science concepts encountered in the activity.

How This Book Is Organized

The sections of this book are organized to reflect a natural division of the world of science for the young child.

Scientific Methods: These activities deal with the working world of science. Process skills are introduced and practiced. Tools of science are examined, scientific ways explored.

Family Science: This is a rather special section that will help you plan some activities that can be used for family nights at school or as home assignments to foster parent/child experiences in learning.

My Body: School-age children are always interested in themselves and that wonderful, mysterious and fascinating structure they inhabit—their bodies!

My Earth and Its Neighbors: From soil to solar system, these activities help young children explore their environment—local to universal.

Living Things: The sciences of botany and zoology are represented here along with their natural companion, ecology. Again, these activities are designed to show living things in a way that is relevant and personal to the young child.

The Way Things Act: Physics and chemistry are the basic sciences that explain so much of what we experience. From gravity to floating, this section contains activities that explore the basic concepts of science.

The fostering of scientific curiosity in the young child is a noble thing, and you are to be admired for your efforts. It is hoped that this book will provide you with as much pleasure as it will your students.

Happy Sciencing!

Beverly Hartman

1. An Eye Tool

Outcome
Students will learn to use a tool of science, the magnifying lens.

Materials
For each student (or each group of students):
- magnifying lens (10X) or hand-held illuminating microscope (30X)
- 2 coins (1 new, 1 used)
- tissue
- items common to your area (sand, wheat head, seashell)
- bug
- newspaper square
- leaf

Engage Activity
Assemble a display of tools that are representative of different occupations. Examples: hammer and saw (carpenter), stethoscope and tongue depressor (doctor). Discuss how each thing helps people do their jobs.

Experimenting/Observing
Let children look at everything you have provided with the magnifying lens. Give them plenty of time for this activity. They may need to look at things for a long time and examine every inch. Let them trade items back and forth with each other. Let this be a group discovery time.

Science Notes
Magnification, from hand lenses to electron microscopes, extend our abilities to observe matter. This is one of the first tools used by scientists. Magnification is also used in astronomy to bring the universe closer to the observer. The use of lenses and reflecting mirrors is more complex in a telescope than in a microscope. All are tools of science and their use has opened up opportunities for greater understanding in science. A magnifying lens is a convex lens. Refraction is the bending of light rays as they pass through a lens.

Thinking
Describe some of the things you saw. What were some of the differences between the new coin and the old coin? What surprised you about the newspaper? Can you draw a picture of the leaf that you saw when you looked through your eye tool (magnifying lens)?

Explanation
Magnifying lenses help your eyes to see things in detail that are too small for your own eye. Lenses bend light rays so that things appear larger than they really are.

Extension
Drawings or word descriptions that can be shared with other classes or family are a natural extension of this activity. Compare and contrast what you can see with the eye and then with the "eye tool."

2. Observe This!

Outcome
Students will practice skills in scientific observation.

Materials
- signs for LOOK, SMELL, TOUCH, TASTE, HEAR
  (for nonreaders use drawings of eyes, finger, nose, tongue, ear)
- smell: vinegar and fresh cinnamon stick
- taste: sugar and salt (in mini piles on wax paper)
- touch: sandpaper and velvet or silk cloth
- sight: window of classroom
- hear: whistle and hand clap

Engage Activity
Ask students how they think scientists gather information. List the ways we learn about the world on the chalkboard. Ask students how they can be like scientists.

Experimenting/Observing
Set up stations with the appropriate materials under each sign. After all stations have been visited by all students, demonstrate sound with the whistle and a hand clap. Have students describe their observations (as appropriate for your classroom—orally or written).

Thinking
Which observation skill do you use most frequently? What information did you learn from using different observation skills? Can you describe the salt and sugar using other observation skills instead of taste?

Explanation
Although it seems that we use sight most frequently to observe our world, the other senses give us very valuable information. The salt and sugar were white, grainy, felt hard and had no smell or sound. That's observation! NEVER smell or taste a substance unless given permission by an adult. Some substances can poison by tasting them or by breathing in their toxic fumes.

Extension
Continue to observe things in your environment each day until students become quick and efficient observers.

Science Notes
Observation is the first step in good sciencing and should be an education priority in your classroom. All the tools of science have been developed to enhance our observational skills.

3. What Puts the Pop in Popcorn?

Outcome
Students will practice gathering and recording scientific data.

Materials
- hot air popcorn popper
- popcorn
- measuring cups
- balance or scale
- bowl for popped popcorn

Engage Activity
Display as many kinds of balances and scales as you can (examples: bathroom scale, baby scale, fruit scale, digital scale, veterinarian's scale). Have students discuss how each is used.

Experimenting/Observing
Help students learn to use whatever type of scale or balance you have for this activity. Practice helps them gain mastery and confidence in an important scientific skill.

Measure amount of popcorn needed for your particular popper. Weigh that amount of popcorn (weight of container and popcorn minus weight of container). Pop the popcorn. Weigh the popped popcorn (weight of container and popcorn minus weight of container). Record the weights and subtract the weight of popped corn from unpopped corn.

Thinking
Did the popcorn weigh more before it was popped or after it was popped? Can you explain the differences in the weights? What do you think happens when a popcorn kernel pops?

Explanation
Popcorn kernels contain a large percentage of water. When they are heated to a high temperature, the water turns to steam and explodes out of the kernel. The popped popcorn no longer has water in it so it weighs less.

Extension
Compare popping weights of fresh and dried out popcorn kernels. Compare number of unpopped kernels between fresh and old popcorn. Compare brands of popcorn.

Science Notes
When the steam explodes the popcorn kernel, the remaining starch puffs out into the familiar shape of popcorn. Unpopped kernels usually result when the kernel shell has a hole in it that allows the steam to escape gradually rather than building up to a "pop." Dried out popcorn often does not contain enough water to explode the kernel properly.

4. Why Seat Belts?

Outcome

Students will conduct an experiment that serves as a model for a moving car and passenger. They will see why seat belts are necessary in automobiles.

Materials

For each student:
- 4" x 6" (10.16 x 15.24 cm) index card
- penny
- various toys (see below)

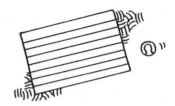

Engage Activity

Display toys that are models for real things that move and/or are used for work (toy dump truck, toy kitchen with pots and pans, etc.). Ask what real things they represent and how the real things are different from the toys.

Experimenting/Observing

Place penny on card. Begin to move the card with the penny as a passenger. Speed up. Quickly stop the card. Watch what happens to the penny. Again move the card with the penny. This time make a turn with the card. Watch what happens to the penny. Repeat these moves until you have seen the penny do the same thing at least three times.

Thinking

This experiment was to show you how things act in real life. What represented a car in this experiment? What represented a passenger in this experiment? What happened to the penny when you suddenly stopped the card? When you turned the card? How could you use this experiment to show that it is important to wear seat belts?

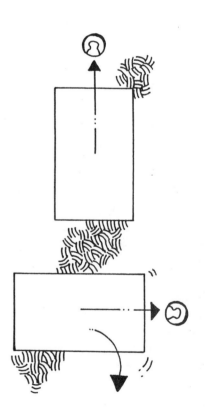

Explanation

The card represented a car, the penny a passenger. When the card was quickly stopped or turned, the passenger continued traveling in a straight line. In a real car, the passenger would have hit a window, the dashboard or the steering wheel. The passenger could be badly injured when this happens. Seat belts keep passengers firmly in their seats so that they cannot keep moving when the car stops or turns.

Extension

Relate this to Newton's law of motion that tells us that an object in motion keeps moving in a straight line until something stops it.

Science Notes

The use of models in science helps us to observe and understand phenomena that occur in time and space that we cannot easily see or manipulate. A tornado in a tube is a scientific model. Structures representing atoms are scientific models. Much of science is too small, too large or too wild to observe and experiment with in person. We are now seeing wonderful models of science for the public in zoos and oceanariums when they provide mini habitats for exotic animals and plants.

5. A Many-Tone Twanger

Outcome
Students will identify different sound tones as being high or low. They will see the connection between speed of vibration and tone produced.

Materials
For each student or group of students:
- ruler (plastic or wood) or wooden paint stirring stick
- book
- desk edge

Engage Activity
Have students place their hands gently over their voice boxes while they hum high and low notes.

Experimenting/Observing

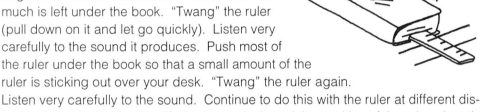

Put the book at the edge of your desk, slip the ruler under the book so that it hangs over the edge of the desk. Pull the ruler out so that not much is left under the book. "Twang" the ruler (pull down on it and let go quickly). Listen very carefully to the sound it produces. Push most of the ruler under the book so that a small amount of the ruler is sticking out over your desk. "Twang" the ruler again.
Listen very carefully to the sound. Continue to do this with the ruler at different distances from the book. Identify the low sounds and the position of the ruler when those low sounds are made. Identify the high sound and the position of the ruler when those high sounds are made. Observe the motion of the ruler as you twang the ruler.

Thinking
What position of the ruler produced low sound? What position of the ruler produced high sound? What was the motion the ruler made when you twanged it? What was the motion in your voice box when you made low sounds? Could you feel these same motions when you made high sounds?

Explanation
The ruler made low sounds when it was pulled out at least half of its length from the book. The high sounds were produced when the ruler was very close to the book. When you twanged the ruler, you made it vibrate. These vibrations are responsible for sound. The slow vibrations from a long section of ruler produce low sounds. You could feel these vibrations in your throat when you made low sounds. High sounds are made when the vibrations are very quick. This happened when the ruler was close to the book. They are hard to see and hard to feel in your throat, too.

Extension
Invite someone to demonstrate high and low notes on a stringed instrument for your class. Make the connection between length and speed of vibration. Longer, slower, lower. Shorter, quicker, higher. Larger instruments—longer strings and lower sounds.

Science Notes
The muscles that control the vocal cords can control the amount of vocal cord that is allowed to vibrate. Producing low tones means a great deal of each vocal cord is vibrating. Because it takes longer to vibrate the longer cord, the rate of vibration is slower. The opposite is true for higher sounds. Puberty brings a lengthening of the vocal cords in males, thus the lower tones of men's voices. Singers increase their range of high and low sounds with practice. The muscles that control the vocal cords benefit from training just as the muscles for an athlete or dancer.

6. Weird Ice Cubes

Outcome
Students will describe their observations in an experiment dealing with an acid/base indicator.

Materials
For the classroom:
- cabbage juice ice cubes (You will need enough for each student or group of students to have three cubes. Preparation: Chop up red cabbage leaves and put in blender. Pour in hot water. Blend. Drain off juice and put in ice cube trays. Freeze until experiment time.)

For each student or group of students:
- 3 tall, plastic drinking glasses
- lemon juice
- baking soda
- water
- plastic spoons

Engage Activity
Have students close their eyes while you describe your kitchen at home in great detail. Afterwards, discuss what they remember from your word description. Discuss the role of description in science experiments. Word descriptions are how scientists tell each other what they have seen, felt, smelled and measured.

Experimenting/Observing
Pour water into each of the three glasses. Add 4 spoonfuls of lemon juice to one glass and stir. Add 4 spoonfuls of baking soda to another glass and stir. Describe the appearance of each glass. Describe the weird ice cubes that your teacher will give you. Put one ice cube in each glass. Describe the changes that happen in each glass. After the ice cubes have completely melted, describe the contents of the glass again.

Thinking
What was different about the glasses before you added the ice cubes? What was different about the ice cubes? What happened when you added the ice cubes to each glass? What did the glasses look like after the ice cubes had melted?

Explanation
The glasses should have all looked like water. The ice cubes were purple rather than clear like regular water ice cubes. The liquid in each glass began to turn a different color when you added the ice cubes. The glass with the lemon juice turned to a pinkish color. The glass with the baking soda turned to a blue-green color. This happened because the ice cubes were made of red cabbage juice which indicates the presence of acids and bases by changing colors. Substances that are acid turn pink, and substances that are base turn blue or green. Substances that are neutral (neither acid nor base) stay purple like the cabbage juice. Red cabbage juice is called an acid/base indicator.

Science Notes
Chemical indicators are substances that will turn a different color in the presence of an acid or a base. Chemical indicators are a first test when trying to determine the identity of an unknown substance. There are many chemical indicators with a varied range of information they can indicate. Luckily for us, cabbage juice is cheap and easy to obtain and remarkably sophisticated in the information about acids and bases it can give us!

7. How Much Silly into the Putty?

Outcome
Students will make a polymer putty substance by carefully measuring the ingredients.

Materials
Protect work area surfaces with butcher paper. Have ready for each student or group of students:

- low-profile plastic drinking glasses
- plastic spoons
- small plastic bag
- cookies and recipe (see below)
- wooden craft sticks
- Elmer's Glue-All® (use fresh glue)
- Purex Sta-Flo® liquid starch

Engage Activity
Have all the ingredients for a recipe of cookies on display along with samples of the baked cookies. Ask students to direct you in putting together another batch of cookies. Take this opportunity to stress that you need more information than just *what* goes into the cookies. You need to know *how much* of everything goes into the cookies. Explain that science does not like "naked" numbers. Numbers must have labels. In your recipe you could not add 3 flour, it had to be 3 cups of flour. Exact measurements ensure good science results.

Experimenting/Observing
Put 12 spoonfuls of glue into a glass. Add 6 spoonfuls of liquid starch. Stir them together with the wooden stick. When it becomes too hard to stir, take the mixture out of the glass and put it in your hand. Knead it for a while until it acts like putty. If the mixture gets sticky, have someone put a few drops of starch into your hand and keep kneading it. Save the putty in the plastic bag.

Thinking
Were you successful in making putty? Why do you think you were successful? Do you think you could have made it by using 6 spoons of glue and 12 spoons of starch? Why is it important to measure things?

Explanation
There are many recipes in science. One of them is for the putty you made. If you do not follow recipes, you do not end up with the substance that you want. If you switched the amounts in the putty, you would end up with a mess. Measurements in science are also important for gathering information that is accurate. How many inches (centimeters) the plant grows each day would be an important measurement in science.

Extension
If appropriate, let students work out the recipe for themselves by trial and error. The ratio of this putty is simple: 2 parts glue and 1 part starch. Putty is a non-Newtonian substance. Refer to activity "Marvelous, Messy, Mysterious Science!" (page 15) for a discussion of these substances.

Science Notes
There is a fine line to walk in science education between making it seem so exacting that it loses its appeal and giving the impression that random muddling about is responsible sciencing. The great advances in science are a combination of creative thinking and concrete/sequential thinking. We want someone to find the cure for cancer and to make sure they write down how to do it! Showing students that following directions can lead to fun sciencing rewards accuracy.

8. Light vs. Paint

Outcome
Students will predict the outcome when they mix different colors of light and paint together.

Materials
For each group of students:
Light materials
- 2 flashlights
- cellophane pieces to cover the flashlights in red, green, yellow and blue
- rubber bands to anchor cellophane around flashlights
- white paper for background to shine lights on

Paint materials
- white paper to paint on
- red, green, yellow and blue paint
- paintbrushes
- paint swatches
- prism

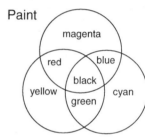

Light

Paint

Science Notes
Colors can come from colored light (television images) or from colored pigments (red rose). When all the colors of light are combined, the result is white light (reverse of splitting white light into colored spectrum with a prism). When all colored pigments are combined, the result is an absence of color (black). A color pigment absorbs all the colors of white light except the one that is reflected back for our observation. An object that is black absorbs all colors and reflects none. Leaves are green because they absorb all white light except green which is then reflected off the leaves.

Engage Activity
Pick up a quantity of paint swatches at the hardware store. Pass them around the room and ask students to guess what colors were mixed to get these various shades. Use a prism to break the sunlight coming into the classroom window into the spectrum that makes up white light. Tell students that they are to predict (guess) what color they will be making before they do each step of the experiment.

Experimenting/Observing
Predict what color you will get when you mix red and green paint. Mix red and green paint. Observe the results. Predict what color you will get when you mix red and green light. Put red and green cellophane covers on your flashlights and point them so that the colors overlap. Observe the results. Predict, mix and observe results for yellow and blue paint. Predict, mix and observe results for yellow and blue light.

Thinking
Were you surprised by this experiment? What predictions did you make that were correct? Which predictions did not turn out? What color do you get when you mix red and green paint? Red and green light? What color do you get when you mix yellow and blue paint? Yellow and blue light? Is there a difference between paint and light?

Explanation
Red and green paint combine to make the color brown. Red and green light will make yellow light. Yellow and blue paint will combine to make green. Yellow and blue light will result in white light. Paint and light are very different. When you mix all the colors of paint together you will get black, when you mix all the colors of light together you will get white. Primary colors of light are red, blue and green. Primary colors of paint (or pigments) are magenta, cyan and yellow.

9. Colors from Colors

Outcome
Students will further their science skills by conducting an experiment in color chromatography.

Materials
For each student or group of students:
- coffee filter papers
- scissors
- washable, felt-tip markers
  (Share markers. Be sure to include
  pastels and other colors that are not primary colors.)
- ruler
- water
- short, plastic drinking glasses

Engage Activity
Discuss science experimenting with your class. Stress that scientists conduct experiments to answer questions and to test ideas they have about science. When students experiment, it is important that they follow directions exactly. Sometimes it is necessary to repeat an experiment just to be sure of what happened. Observing everything that happens is a very important part of experimenting. Sometimes things happen in a hurry, and sometimes they take awhile. You must always be aware of your safety while experimenting.

Experimenting/Observing
Cut strips out of coffee filters that are 6" x 1" (15.24 x 2.54 cm). Cut a point at one end of each strip. One inch (2.54 cm) from the point, make a large dot with a marker in the middle of the strip. Make a strip for each color marker. On one marker, put every color on the dot so that it is black. Put 1" (2.54 cm) water in the bottom of the drinking glass. Slowly lower each strip down the inside edge of the glass until just the point touches the water. Fold the strip over the top edge of the glass. Observe what happens immediately, after 15 minutes, after 30 minutes and after 24 hours.

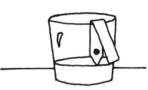

Science Notes
Chromatography is used as a method of separating out the individual components of unknown substances. Chromatography tests are used on fluids and gases. The absorbent materials (example: cotton) and carrying materials (example: alcohol) differ from test to test. Chemicals that differ in their molecular weight soon separate themselves in a chromatography test. The results are compared to known chemicals and identification of the unknown is possible. In this activity, the colors themselves told the story of what had been put together to make the original dot.

Thinking
What did the coffee filter paper point do with the water it was in? What began to happen to the colors? Why was this happening? What did the strips with color look like during the first 30 minutes? What did you see on the strip with the black dot on it? What happened to the dots of color after 24 hours?

Explanation
The coffee filter paper absorbed the water in the glass and sent it up the strip. When the water got to the dots, it carried the individual colors that were used to make the marker up the strip too. Colors are made of pigments which have different weights. The lightest pigments quickly followed the water up the strip. Those that were heavier were slower. Because of this, the colors were separated for you to see. After 24 hours, all the colors had time to go up the strip and the dot was together again as it was in the beginning.

10. Separating Rocks

Outcome
Students will develop their skill in comparing and contrasting by separating rocks.

Materials
For each group of students:
- large container of rocks
- empty egg cartons, muffin tins or similar containers for holding separated rocks
- magnifying lens
- newspaper or butcher paper to protect work area surface

Engage Activity
Display an assortment of rocks. Display each rock while you ask students for various ways to describe it. Let students come up with their own criteria. Compare and contrast the next sample. Make suggestions if it seems appropriate—color, shape, made of one kind of rock or of several kinds, shiny, dull, etc.

Experimenting/Observing
Look carefully at each rock. Use the magnifying lens. Decide what category the rocks belong in and place them in the containers. Make sure each container has all the same kind of rock in it. Show your groupings to other students, explain why you have separated them as you have.

Thinking
What did you use as reasons for separating your rocks? Did everyone in the class use the same reasons? Did you have some groups of rocks that had a great number in them? Did you have some groups where there weren't very many rocks in them? Do you think you could dump your rocks back into a big pile and start all over again with different reasons for separating them? Are there many different things to compare and contrast when you study the rocks found in gravel?

Explanation
Some class members may separate rocks according to color, others according to shape and still others according to size. There are many things to see when you look at rocks. Each reason you have for how you separate them tells something about the rock. Color tells what rocks are made of, shape tells how they have been weathered and size tells how much weathering they have been through. Comparing and contrasting is important in science because it gives us information about things.

Extension
Have students label their containers. After the first sorting, put their rocks back into a pile and pass the containers to another group. Children can learn to compare and contrast according to the criteria of others.

Science Notes
Comparing and contrasting are the steps to take in rock and mineral identification—as a beginner or old-timer!

11. Family Feet

Outcome
Parents and students will work together to gather, measure, record and interpret scientific data.

Materials
- letter to parents explaining family science project (see page 103)
- large sheets of colored construction paper
- felt-tip markers
- scissors
- strips of magnetic tape cut in 1" (2.54 cm) lengths
- chalkboard

Engage Activity
Have students and parents stand up and look around the room at all the people. What differences do they see between the people as they stand (height)? Have everyone sit down and stretch their arms out. What differences do they see now (length of arms)? Ask them to make predictions about feet of all the people in the room.

Experimenting/Observing
Provide materials to each family group. Have them remove their right shoe and trace their right foot on the construction paper with the felt-tip marker. Do this for each family member. Cut out the foot outlines and print the family member's name on the foot. Attach magnetic strip to back of each foot. Have family bring their "feet" to the chalkboard and place along the chalkboard according to size. When "feet" are similar sizes, begin stacking them one above another on the chalkboard. Your finished product should look something like this:

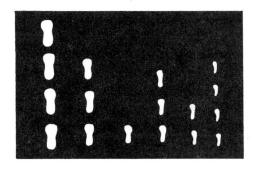

Thinking
What have you made with your "feet"? What conclusions could you make about the sizes of feet in a family?

Explanation
You have made a foot graph! You can see easily how many big feet, little feet and medium-size feet there are in your class's families. Families usually represent a variety of sizes until everyone in the family has reached adulthood.

Extension
Can be done with hands, ears, noses. Feet are the easiest!

Science Notes
Graphs are often used in today's society to give us information. TV, magazines, books and computer printouts present data in graph form that makes it much easier to grasp the significance of numbers. You will have made a graph that should be understood by all! There is great diversity within families and size is one diversity that can be quantified.

12. What Lives in Our Neighborhood?

Outcome

Parents and students will have a new awareness of the diversity of animal life in their environment. Parents and children will work together to gather scientific data.

Materials

- family science night flyers (see page 103)
- pre-printed data sheets (see page 104)
- old magazines
- construction paper
- hole punch, scissors
- felt-tip markers
- yarn
- glue stick

Engage Activity

Display photographs or pictures of animals that are common to your area. Make sure children can identify each.

Experimenting/Observing

Have children construct booklets to take home for observation and data recording by their families. The booklet should include a page for each of the following groups of animals. Discuss each group and their characteristics.

Mammals: Have hair or fur, are warm-blooded, give birth to young and feed them with mother's milk, walk or run using legs.

Reptiles: Have armored or scaly skin, are cold-blooded, lay eggs, can live in water, do not care for young, move by using legs or wiggling whole body.

Fishes: Have scales on skin, are cold-blooded, lay eggs, live in water and do not breathe air, do not care for young, move by using fins.

Birds: Have feathers on skin, are warm-blooded, lay eggs, care for young, move by using wings to fly or two legs to walk.

Amphibians: Have unarmored skin that is smooth or bumpy, lay eggs, do not care for young, live in water during first part of life cycle and move with fins, later live on land and breathe air and move with legs.

Thinking

After talking about the animals in your neighborhood, was there anything that surprised you? Were there more or less "neighbors" than you expected? What did you learn from your family? What did they learn from you?

Explanation

The animal world is usually very diverse in any environment. We live in a world with many other species of animals. When we are observant, we can see many of them.

Science Notes

Ecosystems exist from the frozen Arctic to steam vents deep in the oceans. Many animal species carry out their lives right under our noses! Careful observation can make us aware of their presence and give us a greater understanding and appreciation for the diversity of life on this planet.

Have a Family Science Night

Have families share their results. Give badges (see page 102) to entire family for things such as observing the greatest number, observing the largest or smallest specimen, etc. Be creative so that each family earns an award.

13. Hiding in Plain Sight

Outcome
Parents and children will discover together how camouflage works to hide animals in their environment.

Materials
- family science night flyers (see page 103)
- 18" (45.72 cm) squares of materials in various colorful patterns
- paper dots of various colors made with a hole punch
- items for display (see below)

Engage Activity
Display various military and hunting gear that is made of camouflage material. Discuss why these things are camouflaged. Discuss why animals might want to be camouflaged.

Experimenting/Observing
Provide each family with a material square and a quantity of dots of each color. Have families "sprinkle" dots on their material square. Within a certain time limit, have family members pick up the dots one at a time with two fingers. At the end of the time limit have families construct a graph by lining up dots of the same color. See example below.

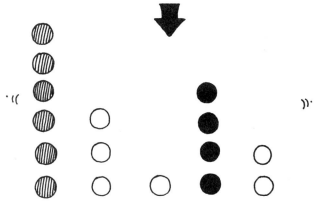

Have each family report on their findings: The color that was most easily seen and picked up, the color that was hardest to see and not often picked up.

Thinking
What colors would be best for feathers of a bird that wanted to hide on your square of cloth? Why? What colors could help an animal that wanted to use color to scare away its enemies?

Explanation
Colors that blend in with the environmental background are used by animals for protection (ptarmigan) or to keep hidden from their prey (polar bear). Patterns can also be used by animals as camouflage. The spotted coat of a baby deer blends in with its background. The use of color and pattern in fur and feathers gives us a glorious array of art in animals.

Science Notes
Camouflage has brought out some of the most clever adaptations in nature. There are mammals and birds that change coloring according to seasons, reptiles and fish that change according to their current background and insects that mimic plant parts. Mankind has used the techniques of camouflage since ancient times to help them remain hidden as they hunted game or to give them an advantage in warfare. Modern military forces use the color and patterns to camouflage everything from uniforms to ships at sea.

14. Recycle and Reuse

Outcome

Parents and children will practice recycling at home. They will find uses for things that are usually thrown away.

Materials

- letter to families explaining this family science project of recycling and making objects for the Throw Away Contest (see page 103)
- large trash bags and a scale for weighing bags
- tables to display items for the Throw Away Contest
- award certificates or badges (make enough for all families)
- margarine tubs (one for each child)

Engage Activity

Have piles of items that can be recycled in your community. Have students wash and remove labels. Make sure they are clear on what to save for recycling. Hand each student a used margarine tub and have them come up with an idea of how they can reuse it.

Experimenting/Observing

Send letters home about your recycling project and contest to find ways to use items that would normally be thrown away. With the input of your students, decide on how you want to spend the money you receive from your recycling efforts. Encourage environmental goals (new tree for the school). During your Family Science gathering, weigh the bags of items to be recycled. Calculate how much money your class will receive (number of pounds times money paid per pound by recycling center). Calculate how many pounds per person of recyclable materials you have collected (total pounds divided by number of people present). Have a member from each family display and explain their Throw Away Contest entry. Judge or vote on the best entry. Be creative with awards—best household use object, prettiest, most inventive, etc. Award all families with ribbons or certificates.

Thinking

Why is recycling important in today's world? Why is it important that we reuse things? What good things happen when you find a new use for something rather than throwing it away?

Explanation

As mankind uses up the natural resources of Earth it becomes essential to learn how to reuse materials in the manufacture of new items. Keeping items in good repair and finding ways to use things that we normally throw away helps conserve resources. Buying items that are made from recycled materials is a wise practice for everyone.

Science Notes

It has become increasingly clear that recycling is essential if we are to safeguard the dwindling supply of raw materials available on the planet Earth. Recycling provides young children with an opportunity to help make a difference in their world. Newspapers, the packaging industry and soft drink manufacturers are leading the way in the use of recycled paper and aluminum.

15. Marvelous, Messy, Mysterious Science!

Outcome
Families will discover the properties of a non-Newtonian substance as they experiment together.

Materials
For each family group:
- ¼ cup (60 ml) cornstarch in 6-ounce (180 ml), low-profile plastic glasses
- 4-ounce (120 ml) paper cup of water
- plastic spoons, wooden craft sticks
- several empty 4-ounce (130 ml) paper cups
- paper clip
- plastic sandwich bag
- butcher paper or newspaper to cover work area

Engage Activity
Have families give example of the states of matter; liquid, solid and gas. Ask how we know the difference between these states of matter.

Experimenting/Observing
Put cornstarch in plastic glass. Add water one spoonful at a time while stirring. You will need about 9 teaspoons (45 ml) or enough to make it glue-like. Have each member of the family poke his finger into the mystery substance with a quick jab. See if the paper clip will "float" on the mystery substance. Divide the mystery substance into the smaller paper cups so all family members have some mystery substance to examine. Pour a small amount into the palm of your hand. Roll it as if you were making cookie dough balls. Then suddenly let go. See if you can break the mystery substance as it pours or when you have it in a ball. Put the mystery substance in the plastic bag to take home.

Thinking
In what ways was the mystery substance like a solid? Like a liquid? Can you think of a name for a substance like this?

Explanation
Because the substance could be broken and you could set the paper clip on top, it was like a solid. When it poured or ran down your fingers, it was like a liquid. This is actually a non-Newtonian fluid. When non-Newtonian fluids are put under stress, they will firm up and break. If there is not much pressure on the substance, it can flow and stretch. Other non-Newtonian substances are quicksand and Slime™.

Dispose of substance in trash can. It will clog the drain!

Science Notes
Non-Newtonian fluids (liquids) are made of long chains of large molecules called polymers. Polyester fabric and PVC pipe are made of polymers. Some polymers occur naturally on Earth–cornstarch and quicksand. Modern chemistry has given us many synthetic polymers. As fluids, some polymers do not conform to the physical properties that Sir Isaac Newton (1643-1727) described for liquids. Non-Newtonian substances will harden when thrown against a wall instead of splashing and splattering They will expand when emerging from a tube.

16. Paper Kids!

Outcome
Each student will see an outline of his or her body. Students will compare their individual heights to the heights of their classmates.

Materials

- paper for cutouts (Using paper from a large roll, cut off lengths that will allow each student to outline his or her body. Splice two lengths together if needed.)
- large-tip, felt-tip pen or crayon
- scissors for each student

Engage Activity
Have a string of cutout kids on display (see pattern on page 106). Explore the following with your students: Does this look like our class? Compare and contrast the kids in this cutout. Predict what a cutout of our class would look like. Read or have children tell the story "Goldilocks and the Three Bears."

Experimenting/Observing

Outline each child with arms and legs in same position as the cutout kids. Have student cut out his or her outline. Have children write their names on one foot of the outline. With student input, arrange outlines from tallest to shortest along one wall of the classroom.

Thinking
What things do you see in each outline? What differences are there between the outlines? What things are the same? Can you predict what the outlines from the sixth-grade class would look like?

Explanation
Children of the same age can be of different heights, but there will be more things that are the same in their outlines. Every outline has a head, arms, legs, torso, etc. People get taller as they get older.

Extension
Have students draw predictions of what the outlines for their families might look like. There are further activities which will require this outline. Laminating them will keep them intact. See page 101 for directions on laminating oversized materials.

Science Notes
All members of the same species have more in common than not in common. Size is one variable, and height one part of that variable. Size is related to age in most species of animals, particularly in nonadults.

17. I'll Huff and I'll Puff

Outcome
Students will see how much air their lungs can hold.

Materials
- boxes of birthday candles, matches
- modeling clay
- 2-liter soda bottle: remove the bottom rim by filling ¼ full of hot tap water, let set until glue is softened, pry off rim with fingertips. Mark bottle with permanent marker at 50 ml increments from bottom to top.
- cardboard square to cover opening of soda bottle
- water
- PVC tubing 20" to 25" (50.8 to 63.5 cm) length
- sink or large tub filled with at least 1" (2.54 cm) water
- alcohol in small bowl

Engage Activity
Line up birthday candles with clay bases about 3" (7.62 cm) apart. Ask for a student volunteer to blow out candles with one breath. Make predictions of how many candles can be blown out. Let as many students try as want to. Make predictions for each student. Ask what they were using to blow out the candles.

Experimenting/Observing
Put water in tub, fill bottle to overflowing. Put cardboard square over top of bottle, invert, put in tub and remove cardboard. (Practice several times so that there are no air bubbles in bottle.) Thread PVC tubing up under bottle and into bottle itself. Have student take a deep breath and blow into tubing until he has "emptied" his lungs. Record the milliliters of air in bottle. Sterilize end of PVC tubing in bowl of rubbing alcohol, rinse and dry. Repeat this experiment for each student.

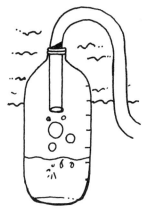

Thinking
Were you surprised at how much air your lungs could hold? Will your lungs hold more air as you grow? Do you think athletes have larger or smaller lung capacity than most people?

Explanation
Your lungs hold enough air to supply your size body with oxygen between breaths. Your lungs grow as you do. Athletes have a greater lung capacity because muscles demand more oxygen during movement.

Extension
Compare different age groups in your school. Compare different size adults in your school. The effects of tobacco smoking, air pollution and lung diseases can be explored.

Science Notes
This activity depends on the fact that air is less dense than water and will rise to the top of the bottle. The air pressure then forces an equal amount of water out of the bottle.

18. Building a Lung Machine

Outcome
Students will discover the mechanism by which we breathe by building a model of the lungs and diaphragm.

Materials
- plastic soda bottle with bottom fourth removed (Use the hard plastic shell as a guide for cutting. This should be done by an adult.)
- balloon
- modeling clay
- masking tape
- plastic drinking straw
- half of a freezer bag
- scissors

Engage Activity
Have students lay on their backs and observe what happens to their chest and stomachs when they breathe. Have them place their hands on their stomachs and breathe so that their stomachs rise. Ask how this helps fill their lungs with air.

Science Notes
The large sheet of muscle that separates your chest cavity from your abdominal cavity is called the diaphragm. As the diaphragm moves up and down, it changes the size of the chest cavity and will either force air out of the lungs (expiration) or draw air into the lungs (inspiration). Respiration (breathing) is usually automatic (like the heartbeat), but we can override the system and breathe when we choose. The rate of respiration is related to the carbon dioxide levels in the blood.

Experimenting/Observing
Cut the plastic bag in a big circle. Sit the soda bottle bottom on top of the plastic bag, bring up the sides of the bag and tape them to the bottle. It does not have to be tight across the end of the bottle but must be taped to the sides so that it is airtight. Blow up your balloon several times so that it is "broken in." Pull the balloon neck over one end of the straw. Tape tightly. Lower the straw and balloon into the bottle top a few inches (centimeters). Put modeling clay around the straw and mouth of the bottle to make an airtight seal. Make a handle of tape and place it in the middle of the plastic bag at the bottom of the bottle. Gently pull down on the handle. Observe the balloon. Gently push up on the plastic bag. Observe the balloon.

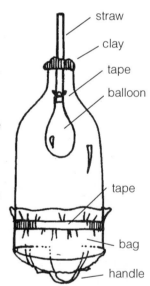

straw
clay
tape
balloon
tape
bag
handle

Thinking
What happened to the balloon when you pushed up on the bottom? What happened to the balloon when you pulled down the plastic bag? What does the balloon represent in your body? What does the plastic bag represent in your body? What does the straw represent in your body?

Explanation
The balloon deflated when you pushed up on the bottom because the air was forced out and up through the straw. The balloon inflated when you pulled down on the bottom because there was more room in the bottle, and so the air rushed down the straw to fill in the space. The balloon represents your lungs. The plastic bag represents the muscles you use when you breathe.

19. A Taste Map of Your Tongue

Outcome
Students will discover that the tastes of bitter, sweet, sour and salty are located at specific spots on the tongue.

Materials
For each student:
- 4 small containers
- lemon juice
- strong coffee
- map of tongue
- strong sugar water
- strong salt water
- glass of water for drinking
- pencil

Engage Activity
Make a class list of all the tastes your students think of. Give them a map of the tongue and explain that they will be testing the four tastes that the tongue is capable of and where on the tongue the taste registers.

Experimenting/Observing
Fill each of your containers with a small amount of either coffee, salt water, sugar water or lemon juice. Dab your finger in one container and then on one of the taste spots of your tongue. Continue doing this until you find a spot where you can taste the substance. Swish some water around your mouth and swallow it. Record that taste on your tongue map. Test all the other containers the same way. Complete your tongue map.

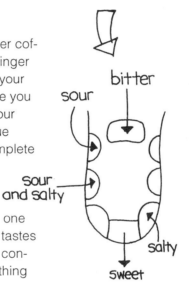

Thinking
Could you taste some of the substances on more than one area of your tongue? Which tastes were they? Which tastes were located in only one spot on your tongue? Which container had something sweet? Something sour? Something bitter? Something salty?

Explanation
The tastes that your tongue can tell you about are sweet, sour, bitter and salty. Sweet tastes are on the front of your tongue, bitter tastes on the back of your tongue, sour and salty on the sides of your tongue.

Extension
Students can test one another with eyedroppers and blindfolds. Have students hold their noses closed for more exact testing. Let all students taste spoonfuls of chocolate and strawberry ice cream while holding their noses and closing their eyes. All they will taste is sweet!

Science Notes
The tongue is only capable of four tastes. There are specialized receptors located in the taste buds of the tongue. These send impulses to the brain and these impulses are translated to us as sweet, sour, salty or bitter.

20. An Important Nose Job

Outcome
Students will discover the role that smell plays in the tasting of food.

Materials
For each group of students:
- shredded carrots, apples, potatoes and pears (all raw)
- plastic spoons
- blindfold
- data sheet (if age appropriate)

Engage Activity
The activity "A Taste Map of Your Tongue" (page 19) will help your students understand that something else besides the tongue must help in our sense of taste. Ask students to share stories about how food tastes when they have a cold.

Experimenting/Observing
It is most important for you not to peek through the blindfold or to use your sense of smell during this experiment! Have one student in your group put on the blindfold and hold his nose tightly closed. Using a clean spoon, give him a small taste of the carrots, apples, potatoes or pears. Have student guess what it is that he has just tasted. Repeat until he has tried all the substances. Change to another taster until all students have had a turn. Now taste everything with your eyes and noses open!

Thinking
What surprised you about this experiment? Was it as easy as you thought it would be to guess what you were tasting? Could you tell if something was sweet, sour, bitter or salty? What information do you think your nose tells you about the taste of a substance? How does your nose and its sense of smell protect you from eating things that could harm you? How does it protect you in other ways?

Explanation
When you have a cold it is hard to enjoy eating because you can't smell your food. Our sense of smell tells us important information about what we are eating. Our tongue only tells us if it is sweet, sour, bitter or salty. The apples and pears were sweet because they are made of stored sugar. The carrots and potatoes are made of stored starch and probably didn't have any taste. Your nose can warn you of food that doesn't smell right because it has begun to spoil. Our nose also recognizes other dangers like the smell of smoke or strong chemicals that could harm us. Although noses are very sensitive, we only recognize smells we already know about.

Extension
Alter appearance of food by adding food coloring. Sight is important in tasting too—remember the story about green eggs and ham!

Science Notes
Humans have the ability to identify up to 10,000 smells. Any tastes that we perceive besides sweet, sour, bitter and salty are the result of olfactory messages picked up from the odors of the food we eat. Because the odors travel up the throat passage to smell (olfactory) receptors located deep in the nasal cavity, it is easy to confuse taste and smell. Unlike our other senses, we find it hard to describe smells with an exacting vocabulary.

21. Sensitive Skin

Outcome
Students will discover that different areas of the body have different sensitivity.

Materials
Students must work in pairs.
- 3 sharpened pencils (tape two of them together so that sharpened ends are even with each other)
- blindfold (optional)
- data sheet with two outlines of human body, front and back

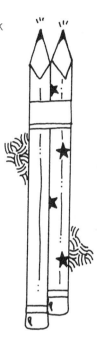

Engage Activity
Discuss with students the sense of touch and what information their brain receives because of this sense. Tell students that they will be doing an experiment to see if all parts of the human body are equally sensitive.

Experimenting/Observing
Put blindfold on one student, or have that student tightly close eyes and keep them closed for experiment. Gently touch student with either two pencils or one pencil. Have her tell you how many pencil points she felt. If she was correct, mark a *Y* on your map. If she was incorrect, mark an *N* on your map. Test areas several times. Make sure that these places are tested: lips, upper arms, fingers, back of the knee, back and feet. Switch jobs so that everyone is tested.

Thinking
Which part of your body outline has the most *Y*s? Which part has the most *N*s? Were you surprised at any of your results? Why would your lips and your fingertips be the most sensitive? Why would your back not be as sensitive as other parts of your body?

Explanation
Your hands and face are the most sensitive parts of your body because they are used in gathering information about what is going on around you. Without a great sense of touch you could not swiftly and efficiently eat your food. Your fingertips are responsible for doing the jobs that require intricate muscle movements. Your sense of touch tells your brain enough information to get the job done. Your upper arms, back, legs and feet do not need to gather as much information.

Extension
Your sense of touch helps you to identify many qualities: sharp/dull, hot/cold, soft/hard, wet/dry, bumpy/smooth, etc. Discuss these attributes (and any others you can name); think how you could determine these qualities *without* using touch; think of items appropriate to each category.

Science Notes
The nerve endings that detect touch are spaced close together in sensitive areas of your skin. You may have trouble locating the exact spot that itches on your back because those nerve endings are so far apart. Our bodies use touch as an early warning system for danger—hot items are dropped, etc.

22. Brrr . . . Cold Fingers

Outcome
Students will experience the loss of feeling and dexterity that result from fingers exposed to low temperatures.

Materials
Have students work in pairs.
- bowl large enough to hold ice, water and student's hand
- ice cubes (lots)
- toothpicks (30 or more)
- water
- paper and pencil

Engage Activity
Have a photograph or picture of a native of the Arctic region. Discuss with students the clothing that is worn and the reason for choosing this clothing. Let students know that they will be experiencing for themselves the effects of cold.

Experimenting/Observing
Mix ice and water in bowl and stir it around until very cold. Have one person stick his hand in the ice water and keep it there as long as he can stand it. Use right hand unless he is left handed—then use the left hand. After he removes his hand from the water, gently pinch both forefingers until it begins to hurt one finger. Record which finger felt pain first. Spread out 30 toothpicks on the surface of your desk. Have student with the cold hand see how many he can pick up in one minute. Record the number of toothpicks that were picked up. Compare the color of the cold hand to the warm hand. Repeat all the steps for the next student. When all your hands are nice and warm again, repeat pinching and picking up toothpicks and record your results.

Thinking
Were your fingers more or less sensitive when they were cold? What was your proof? Why was it so hard to pick up the toothpicks with cold hands? Did you notice any difference in the color of your hand when it was cold? Do cold hands hurt?

Explanation
The cold temperature makes our fingers less sensitive to pain and less efficient in sending touch messages to our brain that help with manipulating objects. Cold hands turn pink when they first become cold because the blood is rushing to the surface to help warm the skin. As fingers become cold they hurt to warn us to protect ourselves. They can become so cold they don't feel anything, and then we are in danger of frostbite.

Extension
Data results can be graphed. Other feats of manual dexterity can be tried—tying a shoelace, buttoning a shirt.

Science Notes
Blood vessels constrict away from the skin leaving it pale when tissues are cold enough to freeze.

23. My, What Pretty Teeth You Have!

Outcome
Students will discover what kind of teeth are in the human mouth and how each tooth type is used.

Materials
For each student or pair of students:
- soap, water and paper towels for washing hands
- plastic knife
- rounded rock for grinding (washed rocks!)
- 2 cookies
- flashlight
- mirror
- food samples (see below)

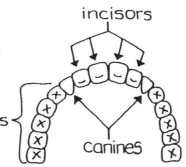

Engage Activity
Have samples of baby formula, baby food, junior baby food and a sandwich. Discuss when each of these things would be given to a child. Lead students to the conclusion that what we can eat is determined by our teeth. Explain that this activity will help them find out what type of teeth we have and what different things these teeth types do.

Experimenting/Observing
Make sure your hands are very clean at all times. Wash them before and after you have put fingers in your mouth. Take the knife and cut the cookie into four pieces. Take the rock and grind one of the cookie pieces. Look at your front teeth in the mirror. Use your finger to feel their edges. Using these teeth, bite one piece of your cookie into two pieces. Look at your back teeth in the mirror. Use your finger to feel their surfaces. Using these teeth, crush one piece of your cookie. Find four teeth in your mouth that do not look like the front teeth or the back teeth. Eat the next cookie. Pay close attention to which teeth you use as you eat it.

Thinking
Do you have teeth that you can use like a knife? Do you have teeth that you can use like a grinding rock? Why do you need different kinds of teeth? Do the other four teeth remind you of teeth you have seen in animals?

Explanation
Our front teeth are used to bite and chop and are called incisors. The teeth next to them that look like fangs are called canines. They are used for ripping and tearing (and we don't use them very much!). The back teeth are used for crushing and grinding. They are called molars. When you have all your adult teeth, you will have 32 of them!

Extension
Simplify terms if appropriate. Have a simple chart of the teeth and have students identify tooth types.

Science Notes
Teeth are the first step in preparing food for digestion. Children have a set of 20 baby (or milk) teeth. The enamel covering on the exposed part (the crown) of our teeth is the hardest substance in our bodies. Adult teeth are firmly set into the jaws with roots. The wear pattern of teeth in ancient skulls can give clues to paleontologists about the age and diet of the individual.

24. My, What Long Ear Tubes You Have!

Outcome

Students will observe how sound waves are contained in a tube. They will compare this to the structure of the ear.

Materials

For each pair of students:
- ticking watch
- tape measure
- cardboard tube from paper toweling roll

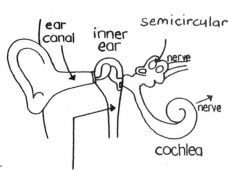

Engage Activity

Make an old-fashioned hearing horn from construction paper. Tell a story about how these were used before we had the technology for hearing aids. Borrow a model of the ear from a doctor's office or draw a diagram of the ear on the chalkboard. Let students study this for several days before you do this activity.

Experimenting/Observing

Students should work in pairs. Hold the ticking watch up to your ear and listen carefully. Slowly move the watch away from your ear until you can no longer hear the ticking. Measure the distance from your ear to where you lose the sound. Hold one end of the cardboard tube next to your ear. Have your partner put the watch at the other end of the tube. Listen carefully to see if you can hear the ticking watch. If you can hear it, measure the length of the tube. If you can't hear it, have your teacher shorten the tube.

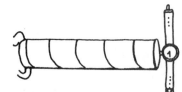

Thinking

Were you surprised by this experiment? What surprised you? How far away could you hear the watch when you weren't using the tube? How far away could you hear the watch when you used the tube? What do you think happened to the sound of the watch when you didn't use the tube? What happened to it when you did use the tube? What part of your ear is like the cardboard tube? How does it help you hear?

Explanation

Sound waves travel through the air and become weaker the further they travel. When sound travels through a tube it does not spread out and is able to keep its energy. Sound must have a certain amount of energy for us to hear it. Your cardboard tube kept enough sound energy for you to hear the ticking watch. Your ear canal acts like the cardboard tube.

Extension

Explore the role of the outer ear in "capturing" sound waves. Build big "bat" ears with paper and see if they improve hearing abilities.

Science Notes

Sound is actually a form of energy that travels in waves which hit the eardrum and make it move. That movement is passed into the inner ear and sent as impulses to the brain.

25. Two Ears to Hear

Outcome
Students will observe how two ears help hearing.

Materials
For each pair of students:

- chair
- blindfold
- noisemaker (something that will be easy for the students to shake for making noise—a rattle, a container with dry macaroni)
- cassette player with moveable speakers

Engage Activity
Borrow and set up a cassette player that has separate stereo speakers. Select a recording that will have obvious stereo aspects to it. Begin playing recording with speakers next to each other. Slowly move them apart. Discuss what students heard.

Experimenting/Observing
Have students work in pairs. Sit in chair and put on blindfold. Partner then shakes the noisemaker in back of the blindfolded partner's head. Have first partner point to position of noisemaker. Let her know if she is pointing to the right position. Repeat in different positions around the partner. Trade jobs so that each partner is able to check his ability to locate sound.

Thinking
Were you able to locate the position of the noisemaker most of the time? What part of your body did you use to help you locate the sound? What helped you most when the sounds were on the left side of your body? On the right side of your body? What did you use when sounds were in front or back of you? How do the stereo speakers use your two ears for a more realistic sound?

Explanation
Your two ears are positioned so that you can collect sound waves from all around you. Sounds to the left are caught by your left ear, sounds from the right by your right ear. Sounds that are in back of you or are in front of you are caught by both ears. If an object is slightly to the left, you will hear slightly more sound in your left ear! In a live musical performance some sounds will come from instruments that are not directly in front of you. Stereo speakers have some sounds come from the right speaker and some from the left—just as if the music were being played in the room with you.

Extensions
Use commercial earplugs to plug one ear and repeat this activity. We do hear some sound through bone, so you will not be able to completely block sound from an ear.

Science Notes
Sound is a form of energy that travels in waves through the air. Our outer ears are shaped to capture as much of that energy as needed for accurate information. The captured energy is converted by the inner ear to nerve impulses that travel to the brain for identification and analysis. When one ear is capturing more energy, or different sound energy than the other ear, we have our own stereo system! This ability to pinpoint sounds is an obvious defense strategy for all animals.

26. Vibrating Voices

Outcome
Students will understand how sound makes the eardrum vibrate.

Materials
For each student:
- balloon
- cardboard tube from paper toweling
- bed sheet

Engage Activity
Let students study a model or diagram of the ear. Arrange students and a bed sheet so that they are holding it like firemen ready to catch a jumper. Instruct them to move their hands up and down rapidly every time you call out a number. Begin counting quickly from 1 to 50. Tell students to carefully observe the sheet and repeat your counting. Let them know that they have made the sheet vibrate. Explain that this activity deals with vibrations that sound produces when it hits a thin, stretched material.

Experimenting/Observing
Inflate and tie balloon. Hold your balloon gently by the fingertips. Use fingertips to feel vibrations in the balloon. Talk softly with your mouth very close to the balloon. Sing or talk loudly to your balloon. Place cardboard tube with one end resting on the balloon, the other end against your mouth. Repeat talking softly, then loudly into the tube.

Thinking
What did you feel when you talked to the balloon? Did the balloon vibrate when you talked through the cardboard tube? What did you produce to make the balloon vibrate? What part of the ear is like the balloon? What will sound do to this part? What was the difference between soft and loud noises?

Science Notes
The eardrum is the first step in changing sound energy into the energy of motion. The eardrum then sets other structures in the ear into motion. Because of the delicacy of the eardrum, it is located within the cranium to protect it. The ear canal must then bring sound energy to the eardrum.

Explanation
The balloon began to vibrate when you talked, and you could feel these vibrations with your fingers. Sound waves hit the balloon's surface and caused it to move (vibrate). Your eardrum is like the stretched surface of the balloon and will vibrate when hit by sound energy. The cardboard tube acts like your ear canal and carries sound energy to your eardrum from outside. Loud sounds cause greater vibrations than softer sounds.

Extension
Set up several balloons in a row touching each other. Using fingers, determine how far different sounds will travel.

27. Balance Your Body

Outcome
Students will discover that their bodies have a sense of balance that tells their muscles how to move to keep them from falling down.

Materials
For each student:
- space to stand against a wall
- tissue

Engage Activity
Have students stand on one foot for a length of time. Have them carefully observe you as you do the same in front of them. Discuss what movements you all made so that you wouldn't fall down. Ask why a high wire walker in a circus usually carries a long pole.

Experimenting/Observing
Find your "space" along a wall and put a tissue on the floor about 18" (45.72 cm) from the wall. Stand against the wall facing the center of the room. Make sure your feet are together and they touch the wall. Try to pick up the tissue without moving your legs!

Turn so that one side is against the wall. Put the foot and cheek of the side nearest the wall up against the wall. Try to lift your other foot!

Turn again so that your back is against the wall. Make sure that your shoulders, backside and feet stay against the wall. Try to jump!

Move away from the wall and try everything again.

Thinking
Were you able to pick up the tissue? If not, why not? Could you lift your foot? If not, why not? Could you jump? If not, why not? Were you able to do these things when you were not standing against the wall? Why?

Explanation
You have something called a "sense of balance." It works to keep you from falling. It tells your muscles where they must move your body to keep everything centered and in balance. When you were against the wall, your sense of balance could not work because it needed to put your arms and legs in the direction of the wall. Your body wouldn't do what you wanted it to because of your sense of balance. When you moved away from the wall, your muscles could move your body anywhere they needed to be.

Extension
Have your principal or other school staff members join you in this activity.

Science Notes
Our center of gravity is a point where it would seem that all our weight is centered. As body positions change, so does the center of gravity. Our sense of balance quickly commands muscles to move so that the weight of our body is evenly distributed around this point. When too much weight is on one side of the center of gravity, we lose balance and fall. These activities use the wall to prevent the body from being able to balance itself. Watching a baby learn to walk is a lesson in how a body develops a sense of balance to accommodate a changing center of gravity.

28. More Balancing Acts

Outcome
Students will discover that their bodies have a sense of balance that tells their muscles how to move to keep from falling down.

Materials
• chair that is straight-backed and armless (for each student)

Engage Activity
See "Balance Your Body" activity (page 27).

Experimenting/Observing
Sit in chair. Make sure your feet are flat on the floor and that your back touches the back of the chair. Fold your arms across your chest and try to stand up. Stand up letting your body move any way it needs to.

While standing up, grab your toes with your fingers. Try to jump forward. Now try to jump backward.

Thinking
Were you able to sit up when your arms were folded across your chest? Where did your head and shoulders move when you did stand up? Were you able to jump forward? Could you jump backward? Why could you go backward but not forward?

Explanation
You could not stand up in the chair or jump forward because your sense of balance wouldn't let you. You could not freely move the right muscles to give your body a continual sense of balance. You were able to jump backward because the weight of your backside helps you keep balanced as you jump backward. When you stood up, your head and shoulders moved forward to keep your body balanced.

Extension
Bring in a toddler and observe his movements. Pick out the times that his sense of balance is not yet developed. Have a dancer visit your classroom. Ask her to walk, sit down and sit up as well as dance. Observe her sense of balance.

Science Notes
The sense of balance is governed by a structure within the inner ear. It contains liquid and quickly informs the brain when the liquid is not level. Muscles respond to bring the body back into balance. A sign of an inner ear infection can be dizziness caused by interrupted messages. The sense of balance in our bodies is the way that our bodies seek to maintain a center of gravity. In a ball that center of gravity is in the middle of the ball. In our irregular forms the center of gravity must constantly change as we change body positions. Arms, legs, shoulders, hips and head all move quickly into positions which keep us balanced as that center of gravity changes.

29. Two Eyes Are Better Than One

Outcome
Students will discover how the vision from two eyes helps them in knowing the exact location of objects.

Materials
• pencil for each student

Engage Activity
Have students close one eye and move the pencil in an arc in front of them. Repeat with opposite eye closed. Repeat with both eyes open. Have them pretend that the pencil is something they are supposed to catch. Have students predict which scenario is more likely to bring them success.

Experimenting/Observing
Close one eye tightly. Hold arms out in front of you with forefingers pointing in toward each other. Bend elbows so that your arms are closer to your body. Move forefingers toward one another so that they touch. Repeat, changing which eye is closed. Repeat, leaving both eyes open.

Thinking
Did this activity surprise you? Did you have trouble getting your fingers to meet with one eye closed? Was it easier when both eyes were open? Why do you think it helps to have both eyes open?

Explanation
When you have one eye closed you only have information about the location of your fingers from one spot. This is not enough information to put two small objects (your fingertips) together. When you use both eyes, you receive information about the location of your fingers from two spots. That information helps you locate things with more accuracy.

Extension
You can try putting the cap on a felt-tip marker instead of touching fingers. Your students may want to try other tasks one-eyed. More exacting tasks will be affected.

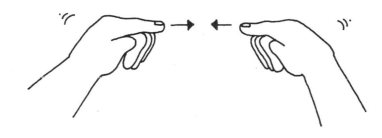

Science Notes
The slightly different views of an object give your brain more information to compute the exact location of the object. This increased accuracy is important to predators who usually have only one chance to pounce for their dinner. Animals (including man) do learn to compensate for the loss of vision in one eye.

30. A Look at Eye Parts

Outcome

Students will observe the parts of the eye that they can see and the purpose for those parts. They will watch the action of their pupils and the reason for that action.

Materials

For each student:
- mirror
- drawing paper and pencil

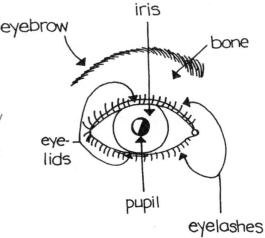

Engage Activity

Borrow a model of the eye and display for several days before you do this activity. Have students generate a list of eye parts that they already know. Discuss ways they could protect their eyes from harm.

Science Notes

A look at a human skull shows just how important protection of the eye is in the scheme of human anatomy. Prehumans had even more pronounced brow ridges than modern man. Our eyes are set in the front of our faces because we are predators, i.e., we need to see what is in front of us to catch dinner. Eye reflexes make it almost impossible not to close your eyelids as something nears your eye. It would be appropriate at this time to discuss what further precautions we take to protect our eyes in today's world.

Experimenting/Observing

Using your mirror, look at one of your eyes and where it is located in your face. Feel the bone that surrounds your eye. Try to figure out how big the hole is that holds your eye. Look at your eyebrows, what they are made of and where they are placed on your face. Look at your eyelashes. Decide which ones are longest. Locate the iris of your eye. It is the colored part. Locate the pupil of your eye. It is the dark, round spot in the middle of your eye. Note how small it is. Squint your eyes so they are almost closed and watch the pupil. See if it changes size. Locate your upper and lower eyelids. Decide which is bigger. Gently pull down your lower eyelid and look for tiny red squiggles in the white part of your eye. Draw what you have seen. Label the different parts.

Thinking

What parts of your eye help protect it? What are they protecting it against? What happened to the pupil of your eye when you squinted? Why does this happen? What do you think the red squiggles are?

Explanation

The bones around your eye protect it from things that might hit your head. Your eyebrows and eyelashes trap dirt and dust before they can get into your eyes. The pupil of your eye lets light into the eyeball itself. It must open wide when there isn't much light (when you squinted) and become small when there is lots of light. Your eyelids protect your eye as well as putting liquid on it whenever you blink. The red squiggles are tiny vessels that have blood in them.

Extension

Turn off lights in the classroom for several minutes. Have students ready to look at their pupils when you turn it back on. Bright lights are uncomfortable until the pupil constricts.

31. Detecting Starches and Fats

Outcome
Students will test foods to see if they contain starch or fat.

Materials
For each student or group of students:
- iodine solution (from drugstore)
- paper from brown paper bags
- half slice of white bread
- several grains of rice
- pat of margarine
- paper toweling to protect desktops if necessary
- toothpick
- slice of raw potato
- soda cracker
- peanut (unshelled)
- French fry

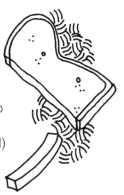

Engage Activity
Have students generate a list of kinds of foods. Display a fast food hamburger. Ask what kinds of food are in this hamburger. Explain that you will be testing foods to see if they belong in the starch group or the fat group.

Experimenting/Observing
Take slice of potato and rub it on the piece of brown paper. Check the paper for a grease spot where you rubbed it. Dip the toothpick in the iodine and put drops on the potato. Observe the color of the iodine after it is on the potato. Write down your observations. Repeat the above steps with each substance you have been given to test except the French fry. Test the outside of the French fry, then break it open and test the inside.

Thinking
What surprised you when you did this test? Which items left a grease mark on your brown paper? Which items changed the iodine to a dark purple or black color? Which substances do you think were starches? Which were fat? What was different about the French fry? How did the potato part of the French fry get fat to surround it?

Explanation
Items that had a great deal of fat in them left a greasy spot on the brown paper. They did not change the color of the iodine. Those items that were starches did not leave a greasy spot on the paper. They did turn the iodine into a dark color. The fats were margarine, the peanut and the outside of the French fry. The starches were the potato, white bread, soda cracker, rice and the inside of the French fry. The French fry had both fat and starch. The fat was added to the French fry when a raw potato stick was put into a pot of very hot oil. Things that are cooked in oil tend to have fat on the outside. People who are trying not to eat any fat can't have fried foods.

Extension
Buy Benedict's solution at the drugstore and follow the directions to test for simple sugars (as in fruits).

Science Notes
Starches are complex carbohydrates (sugars are simple) that are manufactured only by green plants. They are an essential food source for humans. Green plants convert energy from the sun into chemical energy that is stored in all carbohydrates. Our digestion makes that energy available to cells to carry on life processes. Fats can come from plants or animals and provide us with a very concentrated energy source. The fatty acids contained in fats are needed for normal growth and development. Both starches and fats are considered organic compounds because they contain hydrogen, carbon and oxygen.

32. How Quick Are Your Fingers?

Outcome
Students will make a device to test their reaction time in catching a falling object.

Materials
For each pair of students:
- 2 2" x 12" (5.08 x 30.48 cm) poster board strips
- glue stick
- pencil
- ruler
- colored markers
- Nerf™ ball

drop down

Engage Activity
Toss a Nerf™ ball to each student. Have them toss it back to you. Discuss what information their brains had to have to be able to catch the ball.

Experimenting/Observing
Glue poster board strips together lengthwise. Measure down 4" (5.08 cm) from the top of the strip and draw a line across the strip. Measure 4" (5.08 cm) from that line and draw another line across the strip. Color your strip in color bands using the lines as a guide. Have one person hold the strip at its top so that it hangs down between the other person's open thumb and forefinger. The person holding the strip at the top must suddenly let go of it and the other person must try to catch it as quickly as he can. Record the color where it was caught. Do this test several times. Trade jobs and repeat dropping and catching. Record results. Have each person hold and drop the strip with one hand and catch it with the other hand. Record results.

Thinking
Which color on your strip indicated a fast catch? Which indicated a slow catch? Which indicated a medium speed catch? What do these colors mean about your reaction times? How did your speed of reaction change when you dropped and caught the strip yourself? What messages did your brain have to receive and send out for you to catch the strip? What advanced information did your brain have when you were the one to drop the strip for yourself?

Explanation
The color of the bottom represents the fastest reaction time for catching the strip. The middle color represents a medium time. The top color represents a slow reaction time. Your reaction time was much faster when you held, dropped and caught the strip yourself. When your partner dropped the strip, your brain had to receive the information that the strip was being dropped and then tell your muscles to move. When you dropped the strip for yourself to catch, your brain told your muscles to move even before you saw the strip begin to fall.

Science Notes
The time it takes for muscle response to the brain's command for a specific action is reaction time. In the first part of this activity visual sighting of the strip falling is the first step in the chain of events that will result in capturing the strip. The brain must receive, identify and assess the visual clues before directing muscle response. This step is eliminated in the second part of the activity, and the brain simply informs itself of the intent to drop the strip and initiates the command to capture the strip. Like many learned skills, the more often the series of events is practiced, the shorter the reaction time will be for both scenarios.

33. Thumbtack Heart Rate Detector

Outcome

Students will make a device that moves because of their heartbeat. They will see if they can detect a change in the rate of their heartbeats.

Materials

For each student:
- thumbtack
- paper
- scissors
- ruler
- felt-tip marker

Engage Activity

Have students stand and run in place for a few minutes. Make a list of the differences they feel in their bodies after they have exercised. Explain that they will be making a mini machine that will show them how fast their hearts are beating.

Experimenting/Observing

Cut a tiny strip of paper about ¼" (.64 cm) wide and 2" (5.08 cm) long. Fold back one end about ¼" (.64 cm). Carefully stick the folded end onto the thumbtack. Make a fist with your left hand. Feel the cords under your skin that run from your wrist toward your elbow. Find a hollow next to the cords at your wrist on the thumb side. Gently feel in this hollow with the first two fingers of your right hand. If you can feel your pulse, mark that spot with a felt-tip marker. Your teacher can do this for you. Rest your left hand on the table. Place your mini machine on the spot where you felt your pulse. Carefully observe the movement of the strip of paper. Remove the mini machine and run in place for three minutes. Put your mini machine back over your pulse point. Carefully observe the motion of the strip of paper.

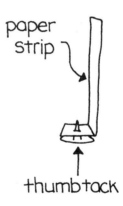

paper strip

thumbtack

Thinking

What was responsible for the movement of your paper strip? What difference did you notice in the movement of the paper strip after you had been running in place?

Explanation

Each time your heart beats it pushes blood through your arteries. You can feel these beats as a pulse. The mini machine used your pulse to move the paper strip. The strip should move faster after you exercise because your heart beats faster to get oxygen and food to your muscles.

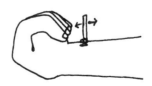

Extension

Have students count the number of times the paper moves back and forth during one minute. This is their pulse rate.

Science Notes

You cannot feel your pulse in a vein because venous blood flow is no longer under the influence of your heart. It is returned to the heart through muscle contractions and gravity. Never take a pulse with your thumb because it has its own arterial "beat" which may interfere with an accurate reading.

34. Discovering Your Voice—Part 1

Outcome
Students will learn how air and their vocal cords must work together to make sound.

Materials
For each student:
- tissue
- balloon
- various whistles

Engage Activity
Gather as many kinds of whistles as you can and blow on each one. Have students identify what you had to do to each one so that it would produce sound. Have each student that can whistle do so. Have class decide what they had to do to produce sound.

Experimenting/Observing
Carefully pull your tissue apart so that you have two very thin tissues. Hold one corner of a tissue between your eyes so that the rest of the tissue falls in front of your mouth. Sing a song and/or recite your name and address. Observe what happens to the tissue as you do this. Remove the tissue. Say your name and address out loud while you breathe in. Blow up your balloon. Let it go and listen carefully. Blow up your balloon again and let the air out while you hold onto the neck of the balloon. Observe what is happening to the neck of the balloon. Repeat this and stretch the neck of the balloon to make high and low sounds.

Thinking
What happened to the tissue as you talked or sang? What made the tissue move? Do we normally talk while we breathe in air? What happened as the balloon deflated? What did the neck of the balloon do to make sound? What could you feel in your throat that was like the neck of the balloon?

Explanation
The tissue blew out as you spoke or sang because we must breathe out to make sounds. Speaking while breathing in is hard to do, and we don't have much variation in sound. The neck of the balloon vibrated when air rushed past it and these vibrations of air produced sound. If you change the shape of the neck of the balloon, you will get different sounds. Your vocal cords vibrate when air rushes past them just like the neck of the balloon. You can feel this with your fingers. Changing the shape of the vocal cords allows us to produce high or low sounds.

Science Notes
The trachea (windpipe) is the tube that carries air in and out of our lungs. The larynx (voice box) is located near the top of the trachea and contains two vocal cords which are flaps of tissue. The muscles that control the cords pull them together as air rushes past them thus allowing them to vibrate and produce sound as a result of that vibration. This is the basic production of sound. The sophisticated sounds of speech are a result of further refinement of that basic sound by teeth, tongue and lips.

Extension
Use woodwind instruments to reinforce the concept of sound as vibrations of moving air.

35. Discovering Your Voice—Part 2

Outcome
Students will learn how their lips, tongue and teeth help produce the sophisticated sounds we know as language.

Materials
For each student:
- mirror
- drawing paper and pencil

Engage Activity
Ask your music teacher to visit the class-room and teach a simple song while stressing correct breathing techniques and enunciation.

Experimenting/Observing
Use your mirror to watch your mouth as you . . .
   recite the alphabet.
   sing a song.
Use your mirror and paper and pencil to . . .
   draw your mouth when you say "O."
   draw your mouth when you say "M."
   draw your mouth when you say "S."
Use your mirror to find the position of your tongue when you . . .
   say "S."
   say "R."
   say "N."

Thinking
What parts of your mouth help form different letters and sounds? Would it be hard to talk without moving your lips? What surprised you about your tongue?

Explanation
Your lips, teeth and tongue help you form the sounds of our language. Ventriloquists can talk without moving their lips, but they must practice very hard to do this. Moving your tongue around in your mouth helps you make different sounds. The tongue is so important to speech that people without tongues cannot talk. When you lose your baby teeth it is harder to make some sounds. When people lose their teeth they get false ones so they can eat *and* communicate.

Extension
Have the speech therapist for your district visit your classroom and talk about his job. Share stories of baby talk and discuss the role of practice in any skill. Try to do some ventriloquism with simple phrases. Mouth "I love you" to your students and see if they know what you said. Talk abut the role of lipreading in people who have trouble hearing.

Science Notes
Speech is a complex skill that mankind has used to pass information between individuals. Speech development was a milestone in the development of man. Current studies look into the ability of other animals to communicate information by sound.

36. Learning from Mud

Outcome
Students will observe the water-holding capacity of different soils.

Materials

- Styrofoam™ cups cut down to 2" (5.08 cm)
- disposable, aluminum pie tins
- squares of cloth to cover cups
- soils samples (example: sand, potting soil, local soil samples)
- water
- rubber bands
- measuring cups
- wooden pencils

Engage Activity
Display watering can, green plants and pictures of floods. Ask students what all of these things have in common. *(water)*

Experimenting/Observing
Pack cups with soil samples. Pour measured water into cup until completely full. Record water amount and soil sample. Cover top with cloth and secure with rubber band. Turn upside down in pie tin. Prop on one side with pencil. Measure amount of water that drains into pie tin. Subtract that from original amount of water added to cup. Record data. Repeat with other soil types.

Thinking
Which soil type held the most water? The least? Which would need to be watered most often if it contained plants? Why do farmers study the soil in their fields? Which soil would hold the most water during times of flood? Which would not?

Explanation
Sandy soils do not hold water very well because water does not stick to the particles of sand. Clay soils hold lots of water because the water sticks to the tiny soil particles. Clay soils retain water better so need to be watered less frequently. Sandy soils need to be watered often. During times of flooding (excess water), clay soils hold much water and become muddy and sticky before they flood. Sandy soils quickly become full of water (saturated) and the water piles up above the ground.

Soil sample in cup

pencil

pie tin

Extension
Test the soil types found in the area of your community.
Compare field soil to riverside soil. Plan a visit from a local farmer or agricultural agent.

Science Notes
Good soils are a combination of sand and clay. Soil that drains well, but not quickly, provides water and then air for plant nutrition. Because sand granules are so much larger than clay particles, the clay particles provide more surface area for water molecules to adhere to.

37. What's in Dirt?

Outcome
Students will see that soil is made of many things by separating the components of soil.

Materials
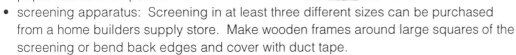

- soil samples
- magnifying lens or binocular microscopes
- paper and colored pencils
- screening apparatus: Screening in at least three different sizes can be purchased from a home builders supply store. Make wooden frames around large squares of the screening or bend back edges and cover with duct tape.

Engage Activity
Have all materials set out on display. Discuss how children could use these things to learn more about what is in dirt.

Experimenting/Observing
Place soil samples on largest screen. Shake to sieve smaller particles through screen. Examine what did not go through the screen. Draw what you see. Repeat with each screen size.

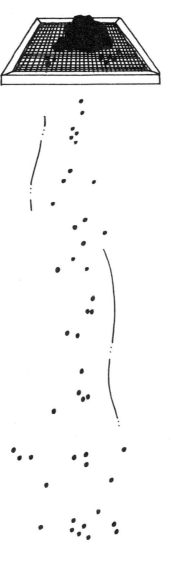

Thinking
What did you see at each level? How many things did you observe in your soil sample besides rock or soil? Were all your soil or rock particles the same size? The same shape? The same color?

Explanation
Soil is made of different things. Since rock is the beginning of soil, you should see rock particles that range in size from pebbles to gravel to sand to silt. Plant and animal parts are called humus. Humus gives soil its dark color and provides nutrition for plant growth. Soil from weathered rock provides elements that plants need to grow.

Science Notes
Fertile soil is the basis for feeding many living creatures, including us. The soil of some Egyptian fields have been yielding crops for 7000 years or more! The weathering of rock materials is responsible for the soil of the earth's crust.

38. A Close Encounter with Sand

Outcome
Students will examine sand to understand its structure and formation.

Materials
- magnifying lens or binocular microscope
- paper and colored pencils
- sand samples: construction sand, beach sand

Engage Activity
Set up a large contained area of your classroom for students to play in the sand. Discuss how they knew it was sand. What does sand feel like and look like?

Experimenting/Observing
Have students put a small amount of sand on a piece of white paper. Using a magnifier and a pencil point, have them spread out grains of sand. Have them draw the different shapes they see. Color the different colors they see. Have them separate the grains by size. Repeat the activity with another sample.

Thinking
Is each grain of sand the same color as all the rest of the sand grains? The same size? The same shape? Do the sand grains look like tiny pieces of rock? How would a grain of sand or a rock become round?

Explanation
Sand can be made of weathered rocks or pieces of coral and seashells. Rock sand is colored. Coral sand is white and is found on beautiful beaches by the sea. If a sand grain is rounded, it has been rolled around in the water until all its sides are worn smooth. If it isn't very rounded, then it has been broken by falling and being smashed. Coral beaches and black lava sand beaches are made by the pounding action of the ocean waves.

Extension
Sands that come from weathered rock usually have a high content of quartz, mica and feldspar. Using a mineral identification chart, identify the components of your sand sample.

Science Notes
Beaches that border the ocean are the result of wave action bringing sand from the ocean floor. Inland sand deposits are usually the result of the weathering of rock formations and the further action of streams and rivers. The composition of local sand will often tell a story about geographic history in that area.

39. A First Look at Rocks

Outcome

Students will discover the great variety of rocks that are found on Earth. They will be able to identify some of the more common types of minerals and rock.

Materials

For the classroom:

- gravel (Obtain several buckets from building contractors of sand and gravel companies—they will usually donate it.)
- tubs with soapy water and water for rinsing, paper towels
- newspaper or butcher paper to protect tabletops
- several bottles of clear nail polish
- construction paper and Scotch™ tape
- labeled rock and mineral samples for:

    Minerals—quartz, mica, feldspar and horneblend

    Igneous rocks—granite, obsidian, pumice

    Sedimentary rocks—conglomerate, sandstone, limestone

    Metamorphic rocks—slate, marble, gneiss
- hammer and towel (to be used by the teacher)
- magnifying lenses and/or dissecting microscopes

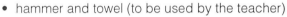

Engage Activity

Display your labeled rock samples for several days before you begin this activity. A handbook of rock identification would be a good addition to your professional library, and students could browse through it at this time.

Experimenting/Observing

Gather several interesting rocks from the buckets. Wash, rinse and dry them. Carefully observe your rocks. Use the magnifying lens. Pick out one rock for your teacher to smash open so you can see the inside. Observe any differences there are in the "opened" rock. Take your favorite rock and see if it contains any of the rock types that your teacher has displayed for

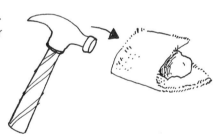

you. Place your favorite rock on a piece of construction paper, and carefully paint it with the fingernail polish. When it is dry, anchor it to the paper with tape. List any rock types that you think are in your rock on the paper.

Thinking

Were you surprised at how many different kinds of rocks there were in the gravel? Did the smashed rock look different on the inside? How? Did you find some rock types from the display in your classroom?

Explanation

There are many kinds of rocks on Earth and many combinations of these. Gravel usually comes from riverbeds that contain rocks that have been washed down from far away. The freshly opened inside of a rock looks different because the materials haven't been exposed to the weather.

Science Notes

Hopefully this activity will begin a lifelong interest for your students. The rocks in your area will give clues to its geological history. Igneous rocks indicate molten rock and possibly volcanic activity. Sedimentary rocks hint at a long ago, shallow sea where rock fragments, shells and bone settled at the bottom until they compacted into rock. Metamorphic rocks suggest great upheavals of the earth since these rocks are formed at great depths under intense heat and pressure. Don't look for diamonds in sedimentary rock, but do look for dinosaurs!

40. Weathering Rocks with Water

Outcome
Students will see the effects of tumbling rocks in water.

Materials
For the classroom:
* buckets of gravel
* tubs with soapy water and rinse water
* large strainers
* water

For each group of students:
* plastic container with snap-on lid
* paper coffee filters
* magnifying lens and/or 30X hand-held microscope

Engage Activity
Collect and display riverbed rocks that are well rounded. Let students feel them and think of ways that they could have become rounded.

Experimenting/Observing
Pick out two or three handfuls of gravel, wash and rinse them. Put rocks in container and fill container one-third full of water. Put lid securely on container so it won't leak. Shake container for 15 minutes. Take turns! Take lid off of container. Observe the water. Place coffee filters in the strainer and pour water through. Let filter dry for a few minutes; then observe what has been caught in the filter with your magnifiers.

Thinking
Why did you wash and rinse the rocks before you began your experiment? What did the water look like after you had shaken the container of rocks? Why did you strain the water? What did you see with your magnifiers? Did you see many colors, shapes and sizes of rock pieces? What would eventually happen to the rocks in the container if you continued to shake it? How does rock tumbling happen in nature?

Explanation
You washed the rocks so that there wouldn't be any dirt getting into the water of the container. The water looked muddy after shaking. When you put the muddy water through the strainer, you caught rock fragments that had broken off your rocks while you were shaking them. You should be able to see rock fragments of all sizes and shapes. The colors will be the same colors that you see in your rocks before you shake them. You could shake the rocks long enough so that they would completely break down into soil. Before that they would become rounded as their corners were broken off. Streams, rivers and waves pounding on beaches do the same thing to rocks in nature.

Extension
Double strain the muddy water to catch the silt.

Science Notes
The weathering of rocks is the first step in the earth's quest to achieve a flat, featureless planet. Water can break rocks by collecting in small crevices and expanding as ice to further fracture the rock. Water chemically weathers some rock types because it tends to be slightly acidic. It is the mechanical action of collapsing hillsides and crumbling banks during flood time along with the merciless pounding of waves and vigorous tumbling of mountain streams that vividly shows the power of water in the weathering of rocks.

41. How High Is a Pile?

Outcome
Students will see the role of gravity in the angle of repose when materials are put in piles.

Materials
Set up several work stations that will include:
- newspaper or butcher paper to cover work area
- large quantities of materials to pile up (Examples: sand, gravel, dried beans, uncooked rice, sugar)
- scoops or cups for students to re-pile the material
- rulers
- paper and pencil for each student
- small rubber balls of various sizes

Engage Activity
Set up a gravity display for the students to explore. Tape rulers together to make slides for different sizes of small rubber balls. Set them up so that they are at various angles—from very shallow to very steep. Let students roll different sized balls down these slides. Discuss what force makes the balls roll down the slides (gravity). Practice drawing slopes.

Experimenting/Observing
Visit each station that your teacher has set up for you to explore. At each station you must:

Pile material as high as you can. Measure height. Draw the slope of that pile. Poke your finger into the side of the pile. Carefully observe what happens to the rest of the pile when you do this. Be ready to describe what has happened.

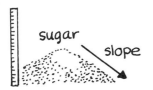

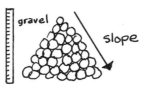

Thinking
What material made the highest pile? Did that same pile have the steepest slope? What happened to the pile height and the slope of the pile as the materials became bigger? What happened to the piles when you poked your finger in the side? What force was pulling down on the material in the piles?

Explanation
Different materials will make piles that have different heights and different slopes. The slope of a pile can be easily disturbed (poking your finger in the pile). If the slope becomes too steep, gravity will make the materials fall down the sides of the pile. When it is disturbed, the pile falls down until everything is stable again.

Extension
Discuss why it is important to be very careful around construction sites where there are piles of building materials.

Science Notes
The greatest slope at which a pile of materials will remain stable is called the angle of repose. This concept is important in engineering and construction. Gravity dictates this angle for various materials.

42. Water—From Here to There

Outcome
The student will construct a model of the water cycle.

Materials
For each student or group of students:
- plastic bowl (margarine tub)
- plastic wrap
- large rubber band
- small container (nut cup)
- water
- penny
- large bowl

Engage Activity
Turn on a faucet and let the water run as you fill the large bowl. Ask students to draw or describe in words the trip that the water has taken to get to the faucet in your classroom.

Experimenting/Observing
Put water in a large bowl. Set smaller container in bowl (weigh down if necessary). Cover bowl with plastic wrap and secure with rubber band. Put penny on top of plastic wrap above the small container. Place in a sunny location. Observe a few times until the smaller container has water in it.

Thinking
What happened to the temperature inside the larger bowl when you put it in the sun? What did you see forming on the plastic wrap? How did it get there? What dripped down into the smaller container? What happens in nature that is like that drip?

Explanation
When the water temperature inside the larger bowl became high enough, the water evaporated (changed into a gas). It then traveled up through the air as a gas until it reached the plastic wrap. There it cooled down and turned back into drops of water. Those drops ran down the plastic wrap to the penny and then dropped into the small container. New water is not normally formed on our Earth; it is evaporated from the surface of the earth into clouds where it then falls as rain or snow. The water you drink today started its journey as it was evaporated from an ocean.

Extension
You can quantify this experiment using temperature, time and water quantities.

Science Notes
The water cycle is one of many cycles we see throughout nature. Pure water molecules are evaporated from the ocean—the salt and minerals are left behind. Water also enters the atmosphere from rivers, lakes and the decomposition of living things. Water molecules are constantly recycled and have been since water became part of the earth's composition. Your sip of water today could contain the same water molecules that were in the soup of a Roman centurion!

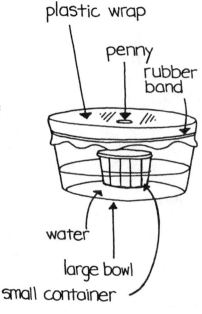

plastic wrap
penny
rubber band
water
large bowl
small container

43. Making a Raincatcher

Outcome
Students will experience the reality of rainfall or snowfall amounts.

Materials
For each student or group of students
- the top 4" (10.16 cm) of 2-liter soda bottle (This can be done beforehand.)
- glass quart (.9463 l) jar
- 6" (15.24 cm) transparent ruler (Make on transparencies and cut out.)
- tape
- paper and pencil

For class:
- large sheet cake pans

Engage Activity
Display newspaper or magazine stories about heavy rain or snowfalls. If appropriate, have students look up record rain and snowfalls. Get a printout from your local weather bureau of the precipitation in your area. Let students look at these displays for a few days before you begin your testing.

Experimenting/Observing

Tape your ruler to the jar. Position it so that the smallest number is at the bottom of the jar. Put your funnel (soda bottle top) into the jar. Set jar outside in cake pans with others from your class. Be sure that they are not under anything that would shield them from rainfall or snowfall. Record how much water is in your jar every 24 hours. If it has snowed, bring the jar indoors and let it melt before measuring.

Thinking
Why did you put a funnel on the jar? Why did you put the ruler at the bottom of the jar? Why do you need to bring snow inside to melt? Why do you need to check the jar every day?

Explanation
The funnel helped catch the rain or snow that wouldn't have made it into the narrowed mouth of the jar. Because the rain piles up at the bottom of the jar, your measuring must begin there. Snow is water in a crystal pattern and takes up more room than just plain water. Five inches (12.7 cm) of snow is NOT the same amount of water as five inches (12.7 cm) of rain. The water that is in the jar will start to evaporate if you do not measure it in a timely manner.

Extension
Compare your readings to those from a year ago. During a rainstorm, let students predict how much rain is falling, and then measure the exact amount from your raincatcher.

Note: Plan this activity during the stormy season in your area! In desert areas convert to measuring sprinklers.

Science Notes
Precipitation occurs when the water vapor in a cloud turns to a liquid (rain) or a solid (snow, hail) and falls to Earth. Precipitation records are kept to help in predicting future weather patterns, to calculate whether a community is facing a water shortage or is in danger of flooding. States that rely on crop irrigation must use rainfall records to divide available water between agricultural and domestic needs. Rainfall and snowfall amounts can tell us about the severity of a single storm.

Experimenting, observing, measuring, recording data, comparing, contrasting, predicting outcomes

44. Trees and Temperatures

Outcome
Students will measure outside temperatures and predict the role of trees in cooling and heating buildings.

Materials
For each student or group of students:
- thermometer
- large piece of drawing paper
- paper and pencil
- colored markers

Engage Activity
Make a visit to the school furnace and/or air conditioner. Have students discuss how their homes are heated and cooled. Ask for ideas from nature for heating and cooling.

Experimenting/Observing
Draw a simple map of the school and school yard. Label all the trees. Go outside in the afternoon and take temperature measurements. You will need to leave the thermometer in place for one minute before you take the measurement. For measurements in the sunlight, shade the thermometer with your hand. Take temperatures in the sun on different sides of the building and under the trees in your school yard. Record these temperatures as you take them. Transfer the temperatures to your map. Decide where trees could be planted in your school yard to help cool your school during the warm months of the year. Draw them on your map.

Thinking
What difference did the trees make in your temperature measurements? What side of your building was the warmest? Which side the coolest? Which side of your building could most use trees to help cool it? Could you use nature to help cool your own home?

Explanation
Temperatures can be lowered as much as 20 degrees under a shady tree. The south and west sides of buildings are usually the warmest because they receive sun during the hottest part of the day. The east and north sides of a building are usually coolest because they only receive the morning sun. Trees planted on the west and south sides of buildings so that they shade the building can help cool it. Landscape plans use trees as nature's natural cooler.

Extension
Examine the role of evergreen shrubs on the north side of buildings to help hold in the heat of the building during the cold winter months. Compare the cost of a tree and the cost of air conditioning during a one-year period. Examine the other benefits of planting trees—esthetic; home for birds, animals.

Science Notes
A passive solar home depends on the placement of windows, deciduous trees and evergreen shrubs to shoulder the majority of responsibility for heat retention and cooling of the residence. During the Great Depression the CCC planted evergreen windbreaks to protect farmhouses from cold winter winds throughout the Midwest. People have been using deciduous trees to cool them and evergreen trees to shield them from the cold for centuries!

44

TLC10002 Copyright © Teaching & Learning Company, Carthage, IL 62321

45. Clouds That Tell the Weather

Outcome
Students will observe clouds, learn what weather conditions they are associated with and create cloud pictures.

Materials
For each student:
- blue construction paper
- cotton balls and/or cotton batting
- white paper and pencil
- glue stick
- scissors

For the teacher:
- chart of cloud types on poster board or labeled photographs of cloud types. See page 105.

Engage Activity
Prepare cloud type chart and display in classroom. For at least a week before this activity, take students outside twice a day to look at the sky. Have them pay particular attention to any clouds. Compare what they see outside to the chart you have provided for them.

Experimenting/Observing
Using your cotton and the glue stick, make a cloud picture that has cumulus and cumulonimbus clouds. Using your cotton and the glue stick, make a cloud picture that has stratus clouds and nimbostratus clouds. Using your cotton and the glue stick, make a cloud picture that has cirrus clouds. Make and cut out the following labels: two that say RAIN, one that says FAIR WEATHER, one that says THUNDER AND LIGHTNING, one that says HAIL, two that say SNOW and one that says DRIZZLE. Glue these labels on the correct cloud type.

Thinking
Have you seen an example of each cloud type? How will being able to identify each type of cloud help you plan what to wear each day? What other ways could it help you to know cloud types and the weather they produce?

Explanation
Unless you live in a desert area, you have probably seen each cloud type. When you can identify cloud types, you can forecast the weather and plan ahead for what you will wear and what you will do outside.

Extension
Continue to keep a weather eye out each day of school so that students will have this ability as a lifelong skill. Compare cloud formations as the seasons change. Look into folk sayings and rhymes about the weather.

Science Notes
Clouds are a step in the water cycle on Earth. Water vapor evaporated from the surface sources collects in clouds for transportation across the countryside. Weather conditions dictate how long a cloud holds its water cargo. Cumulus clouds indicate fair weather. When they develop into cumulonimbus clouds there can be thunder, hail and snowstorms. Stratus clouds produce drizzle and then continuous rain or snow when they enlarge to nimbostratus. High altitude cirrus clouds are driven by high winds and can indicate a change in the weather.

46. Naming the Wind

Outcome
Students will be able to tell the strength of the wind by observing movements of commonplace items.

Materials
For each student or group of students:
- 2-week calendar for recording winds
- copy of modified Beaufort wind strength scale:

Calm	No wind, smoke rises straight up.
Light Breeze	Smoke shows wind direction, leaves rustle, wind can be felt on face.
Moderate Breeze	Raises dust, small branches and paper, flag waves out from flagpole.
Strong Breeze	Small trees sway, large branches move, wind whistles in telephone wires.
Gale	Hard to walk, whole trees in motion with breaking branches.
Storm	Trees are uprooted, buildings are damaged.
Hurricane	Devastating damage, loss of life.

Engage Activity
Display photos of the aftermath of storms. Talk about the winds that students have experienced.

Experimenting/Observing
Every day for two weeks go outside and observe how the wind is moving objects in your area. Check with your Beaufort scale and record the wind terminology in the correct square in your calendar.

Thinking
What kinds of winds did you record during your two weeks? What kind of wind did you record most often? What effect do the seasons have on the winds in your area?

Explanation
There are times of the year when you will record many other kinds of wind besides "calm." At other times of the year you will record "calm" most of the time. Some seasons have stormy weather with strong winds.

Science Notes
Wind is responsible for moving weather. Prevailing winds are from west to east in the United States. Winds from the south usually bring warm, wet weather and those from the north bring cold, wet weather. Wind was important in water travel and still remains important as an energy source. The complete Beaufort scale is widely used.

Extension
Keep a weather eye out all during the school year. If a strong storm moves in, have students observe for wind indications. Teach students to tell the direction of the wind by licking a finger and holding it up in the air.

47. Keeping Track of Shadows

Outcome
Students will observe how a shadow clock can tell the time of day.

Materials
For each student:
- 1 6" (15.24 cm) diameter poster board circle
- new No. 2 pencil, sharpened
- nail
- regular pencil

Engage Activity
Cover the clocks in your classroom for a few days. Keep asking the students if they know what time it is. Have them explain their guesses. Ask how people might have kept time before there were watches and clocks.

Experimenting/Observing
Poke the nail through the middle of your circle. Remove it. Poke the sharpened pencil through the hole. Pick a spot outside where there will be no shade all day long. Gently poke the pencil into the ground so that it is stable. Trace the shadow of the pencil in your circle. Observe the position of the sun in the sky. Leave your circle in the ground. Return every hour during the day and trace the shadow. Each time, note where the sun is in the sky. Bring your circle in at the end of the day.

Thinking
Was the shadow in the same place on your circle every time you went outside? Was the sun in the same place every time you went outside? Was there a shadow at noon? Where was the sun in the sky at noon? What have you begun to make with your circle? How could you completely fill your circle with shadow lines? Would your circle help you tell time if you did not have a watch? Would your circle help you tell time on a cloudy day?

Explanation
As the earth turns eastward in its rotation, the sun appears to travel from the east to the west. This movement is a steady pace so that it travels the same distance each hour of the day. The sun will cause the pencil shadow to be in a different position each hour. Sometimes at noon the sun will be directly overhead and therefore there will be no shadow. If you started your experiment at dawn and marked the shadow for the next 12 hours, you would completely fill your circle. You have made a shadow clock. Similar clocks were used by mankind before mechanical clocks were invented. Shadow clocks aren't much help on cloudy days or at night.

Note: Make circles one day. Begin shadow tracings first thing the next day so that children can get in as many observations as possible during the school day.

Science Notes
The two natural divisions of time on Earth are the day and the year. The sundial was an early (2000 B.C.) and effective device for dividing the day into units that were not obvious divisions. Water clocks and hourglasses that would work through the night were also efforts to bring daily time under some kind of widely acceptable divisions. The development of the pendulum clock in the 1600s finally made accurate timekeeping possible. We now rely on atomic clocks as the standard to which we set all clocks.

48. Sunrise, Sunset and Blue Skies

Outcome
Students will make a model of the earth's atmosphere and discover why sunrises and sunsets appear pink and orange.

Materials
For each student or group of students:

- plastic drinking glass
- milk
- measuring spoons
- prism
- water
- flashlight
- craft stick for stirring
- photographs of sunrises and sunsets

Engage Activity
Display photographs of sunrises and sunsets. Borrow a prism and demonstrate how white light can be broken into a spectrum of different colors.

Experimenting/Observing
Note: The ratio of milk to water needs to be ¼ teaspoon (1.25 ml) milk to 8 ounces (236.56 ml) water. Provide a darkened classroom when flashlights are in use.

Fill glass three-fourths full of water. Shine flashlight through the water from the side and from the back. Observe carefully. Measure correct amount of milk and put into the glass of water. Stir thoroughly with stick. Shine flashlight through the glass from the side. Carefully observe the color you see in the glass. Shine flashlight through the glass from the back toward you. Carefully observe the colors you now see in the glass.

Thinking
Did you observe any colors when the light traveled through the water? After you added the milk, did you see colors in the glass? What color did you see when the light was from the side? What colors did you see when the light was from the back? If the water represented our atmosphere, what did you do to it when you added milk?

Explanation
Light traveled through the water without scattering the colors of the spectrum. The milk scattered the light just as dust, water and pollution do in our atmosphere. When the light was at the side, it scattered the blue part of the light. When the light was at the back, it traveled through enough of the milk to scatter the pink and orange colors for you to see. When the sun is closest to us, we see blue skies. When it is furthest from us at sunrise and sunset, we see pink, orange and red skies.

Extension
Obtain pictures of a sunset after Mt. St. Helens' eruption. The bits of volcanic dust in the air made sunsets spectacular.

Science Notes
The shape of the earth, its rotation and particles in the atmosphere all work together to produce colored sunshine!

49. A Trip Around Earth's Neighborhood

Outcome

Students will understand how a scientific model works to show us things that we cannot observe directly. They will become familiar with the vast distances in our planet's neighborhood—the solar system.

Materials

- adding machine paper
- meter sticks
- pencils

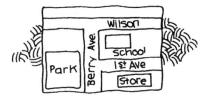

Engage Activity

Have a model of the solar system displayed in the classroom. Draw a simple map of the neighborhood surrounding your school using streets and including several familiar places on the map (stores, parks, etc.). With student help, figure out how far you are from each of these places. Lead discussion to Earth's neighborhood and what large structures are in the solar system. Include Sun, Mercury, Venus, Earth, Mars, Jupiter, Saturn, Uranus, Neptune and Pluto.

Experimenting/Observing

Have students put a dot at the beginning of the tape and label it as the Sun. Measure the planets from this point. Put a dot for each planet and label that dot with the name of the planet it represents. Mercury = 3.9 cm; Venus = 7.2 cm; Earth = 10 cm; Mars = 15 cm; Jupiter = 52 cm; Saturn = 92 cm; Uranus = 192 cm; Neptune = 300 cm; Pluto = 394 cm

Thinking

What group of planets are closest to the sun? Which are the furthest? Between which two planets is there a great big space? Are you surprised at how far Pluto is from the sun? What do you think the temperature is like on Mercury?

Explanation

The inner planets are Mercury, Venus, Earth and Mars. The outer planets are Jupiter, Saturn, Uranus, Neptune and Pluto. The large space between Mars and Jupiter separates the inner and outer planets. Pluto is an icy, dark planet while Mercury is so hot that the atmosphere has been burned off.

Science Notes

Space science relies on models to help us understand the solar system. The planets are not obvious in the night sky and their various orbits make it impossible to see them at one time. Astronomy for a long time was only for the very elite—now most of us are aware of Earth's neighbors from books and television programs. The light from the sun takes 8 minutes to reach Earth, almost 5½ hours to reach Pluto! And light travels quickly enough to travel around the earth 7 times in one second. The distances and sizes in our own solar system are hard to imagine, in the universe they are simply staggering! An awesome subject for young minds!

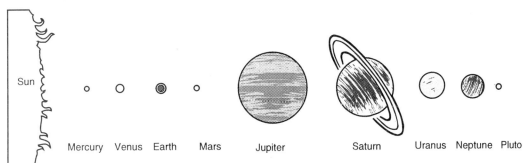

Sun   Mercury   Venus   Earth   Mars   Jupiter   Saturn   Uranus   Neptune   Pluto

50. Making Phases of the Moon

Outcome
The student will use a model to reproduce the phases of the moon.

Materials
- Styrofoam™ balls—at least 3" (7.62 cm) in diameter
- sharpened, wooden pencils
- light source (flashlight, lamp, etc.)

Engage Activity
Ask children to observe the moon for several weeks before you do this activity. Have students describe the moon each day.

Experimenting/Observing
Have students poke end of pencil into Styrofoam™ ball. Have them use the pencil as a handle and hold the "moon" slightly above their heads. Practice turning in a circle, keeping their eyes on the moon. Have students turn so that their backs are to you (the light source). Turn on the light source, turn off classroom lights. Explain that they are seeing the moon phase that is called a full moon. Have them turn a quarter turn towards you. This is a moon phase called a half-moon. Have them face you. When none of the moon is lit by the light source, it is called a new moon. A partial turn away from you will produce a crescent moon. Turning to a position between half-moon and full moon will show a gibbous moon. Let students keep repeating these turns until they understand the phases. (This is much easier than it sounds, but they will need time and repetition for full comprehension.)

Thinking
What represents the sun in this experiment? What represents the moon? Why can you see the moon? Which phase of the moon is the biggest? Which is the smallest where you can still see the moon? Which phase makes the moon dark? Do you know how long it takes the moon to go around the earth?

Explanation
The light source is the sun, the Styrofoam™ ball is the moon. Sunlight lights up the moon so we can see it. The biggest phase of the moon is a full moon, the smallest is a crescent moon. A new moon is a dark moon. It takes one month for the moon to orbit the earth.

Extension
Show large photographs of the moon's surface to your students. The easiest things to be seen are craters (holes) made by meteor impacts. Have children see what they can observe with their own observations of the real moon!

Science Notes
Children are aware of the moon and its different shapes from an early age. There is always a natural curiosity about the moon, and you can take advantage of it. The moon is Earth's only natural satellite, it revolves around the earth in 30 days. In the meantime, Earth is rotating on its axis, taking 24 hours for a complete rotation. The moon is only visible to us for a portion of each 24-hour day. The moon does not rotate so we always see the same side.

51. Water Pipes That Xylem Up

Outcome
Students will see how colored water is transported in plants up their stems to the leaves.

Materials
- stalks of celery with leaves
- quart-size jars
- plastic, serrated knives (if age appropriate)
- food coloring
- water
- potted plants for display

Engage Activity
Gather as many potted growing plants as you can and display them during this series of activities. Label each plant with its common name. Let students help with caring for your classroom botanical garden. Discuss what they need to do.

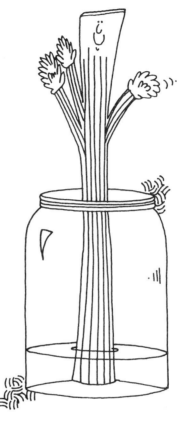

Experimenting/Observing
Put approximately 2" (5.08 cm) of water in jar. Color generously with food coloring. Cut fresh edge at bottom of celery stalk. Put celery stalk into jar. Observe complete stalk hourly during school and then at the end of 24 hours time. Slice celery stalk crosswise every 2" or 3" (5.08 or 7.62 cm) and observe.

Thinking
Why do we water plants? How does the water get from the dirt in the pot to the leaves? What did you see happen to the leaves in your celery stalk? What did you see in the cross section of your celery stalk?

Explanation
All parts of the plant needs water to live, just like all parts of our bodies need water. Roots of plants not only hold the plant in the ground, they take up water and other nutrients from the soil and send them to all the plant parts. The colored water traveled up your celery stalk to the leaves—you could tell this happened because the leaves became the same color as the colored water in the jar. When you cut through the celery stalk you can see the tiny "pipes" that carry water up the plant. These "pipes" are called xylem.

Extension
Starting with several stalks, slice a different stalk at the end of each hour until you discover how far the colored water has traveled in that time period. Vary conditions with warm or cold water and warm or cold room temperatures. Dissect stalk lengthwise to isolate individual xylem bundles.

Science Notes
Xylem tissue is found with the phloem (tissue which carries food down from the leaves) in vascular bundles. These tissues are arranged differently in different groups of plants. The long pipe-like structure of xylem is strengthened with materials that turn into the heartwood of older trees.

52. Watercolored Flowers

Outcome

Students will observe action of plant xylem by dying white carnations.

Materials

For each student or group of students:
- white carnation
- water
- drinking glasses
- food coloring

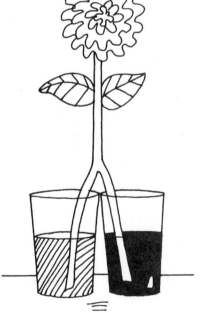

Engage Activity

Show students an artificial flower arrangement or pictures of one. Decide on someone special in your school that the students could surprise. Discuss how they will use their knowledge of science to dye flowers.

Experimenting/Observing

Mix water and food coloring in glass (let students plan this). Snip end of carnation stem so that fresh tissue is exposed. Put carnation in glass. Let stand in colored water until desired coloring takes place. (Amount of time will determine whether color is just on petal edges or if whole flower is colored.) Arrange flowers for presentation.

Thinking

Why did the flowers turn to a color? How did the food coloring get from the glass to the flower petals? What did the flower look like as it was being dyed? Which part of the petals turned a color first? How long did it take to dye your flower?

Explanation

Water travels up the stem of your flower to all the cells of the flower. The "pipes" that carry the water are called xylem. Because water is colorless, you cannot see the water in the petals of the white flower. When you put food coloring in the water, that dye is carried up to the cells of the petal and you see the flower change color. The water moves up slowly so it takes a long time to put enough dye in each cell for you to see.

Extension

You can split the carnation stems part way toward the flower. Put each section in a different color food coloring and you will come up with multicolored flowers.

Science Notes

The xylem tissue of a plant carries water and nutrients that are in solution to all parts of the plant. The food coloring is light enough to be easily transported along the xylem. We use celery leaves and white carnations for these xylem and food coloring activities because they have so little pigmentation in them that the colored water invading the leaf and petal cells is visible to us. Deep green leaves or highly colored flowers would not lend themselves so easily to this activity.

53. Wonderful Water to the Rescue

Outcome
Students will see the path of water absorption by plants and how water is eventually given off as water vapor by leaves.

Materials
For each student or group of students:
• small, wilting potted plant
• water
• plastic bag and twist ties

Engage Activity
Ask students to predict what will happen when plants do not receive enough water. If appropriate in your area, ask students to share stories of drought.

Experimenting/Observing
Observe all parts of your wilted plant and describe its condition. Water your plant so that all the soil around the plant is wet. Wait 30 minutes and again observe your plant and describe its condition. Gently put bag-gie over one leaf of your plant and close tightly with the twist tie. After 24 hours observe your plant again. Describe its condition and what you see in the baggie.

Thinking
What are the signs of a wilted plant? What happened after 30 minutes? What happened after 24 hours? What made the plant begin to "unwilt"? How did the water get into the baggie?

Explanation
When a plant becomes wilted it begins to sag. Water in plant stems and leaves makes them strong enough to stand upright. When that water is gone, the strength is also gone. The plant quickly begins to stand up straighter after you water it because the stem is not very far from the roots which absorb the water and send it up the stem. It takes longer for the water to reach the leaves because they are further away. Water is given off by leaves during photosynthesis. When you see moisture in the baggie you know that there is enough water in the plant for everything to be functioning again.

Extension
This whole activity can be quantified by measuring all the variables—water amount, time, temperature of room. Further experimentation can be done to see exactly how much water is needed to make the cells turgid (filled with water) again. Older students could use this as a jumping-off point for their own experimentation.

Science Notes
Small plants are just fine for this. You might want to practice wilting a plant so that you don't let the plant wilt to the point of no return! A cell with water in it is considered turgid, a cell with a water deficit is considered flaccid.

54. Marvels Within a Seed

Outcome
The students will observe embryo bean plants contained within bean seeds. They will be able to identify parts of these embryos.

Materials
For each student or group of students:
- dried pinto bean seeds (soak overnight in water)
- paper toweling
- food coloring
- toothpicks
- hand lens
- various seeds for display

Engage Activity
Have a variety of seeds, from small to large, for the students to examine. Have students ponder the role of seeds in the life of a plant.

Experimenting/Observing
Carefully "peel" the skin off of the pinto bean seed and split seed into two halves. Repeat with another if necessary until a complete embryo can be seen on one half of the seed. Dip toothpick in food coloring and "paint" parts of embryo. Using your hand lens, identify the embryo leaves (plumules), the embryo root (radicle) and the stored food (cotyledon). Draw what you have seen. Compare your embryo with others.

Thinking
What role does the seed play in the life of a plant? What did you see that surprised you? Where will the root go when planted? The leaves? How will these tiny plants have enough energy to grow into regular plants?

Explanation
Plant seeds contain the beginnings of a completely new plant. Plants must reproduce offspring just like animals. The embryo root will grow down in the soil and the leaves will grow upward to reach the sunlight. The rest of the seed is stored food that the embryo plant uses until its own leaves reach the sun and begin manufacturing their own food.

Extension
Have students compare soaked and unsoaked seeds to see how tough the outer covering is. Use iodine to paint the whole seed half—the cotyledon will stain purple (a sign of the presence of starch), and the embryo will remain pale.

Science Notes
The number of cotyledons determines whether a plant is a dicot (two) or a monocot (one). These are the big divisions in the plant kingdom. Corn and grasses are examples of monocots. Beans, peas and pansies are examples of dicots. In some seedlings the cotyledons grow to the surface and carry on photosynthesis. Cotyledons are also called seed leaves. The endosperm is the seed tissue that contains stored food. In many seeds it is absorbed almost completely by the cotyledons.

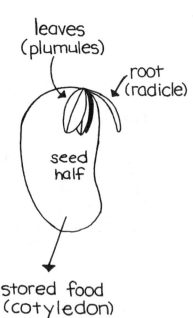

leaves (plumules)

root (radicle)

seed half

stored food (cotyledon)

55. From Seed to Seedling

Outcome
Students will experience germinating seeds.

Materials
For each student or group of students:
- recently purchased pinto bean seeds
- tall, plastic glasses
- paper toweling
- markers that will write on plastic

Engage Activity
The activity "Marvels Within a Seed" (page 54) is a natural lead-in to this activity.

Experimenting/Observing
Soak the bean seeds overnight. Fold paper towels lengthwise and put into glass. Place bean seed halfway down the glass between the toweling and the edge of the glass. Carefully soak the paper towel with water. Place in warm, sunny location and rewater as needed. Mark growth of stem and root each day on outside of glass.

Thinking
What did you give the bean seed so that it could grow? Which way did the stem and leaves grow? Which way did the roots grow? How will this help it become a successful plant? How long did it take for your bean seed to become a seedling?

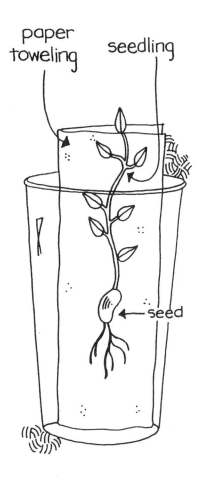

paper toweling   seedling

seed

Explanation
You supplied water, light and warmth so that the bean seed could begin to grow a new plant. This beginning to grow is called germination. The stems and leaves grew upward so that in nature they would reach above the soil and be exposed to sunlight. Plants cannot continue to grow without sunlight. The roots grew downward so that in nature they would reach into the soil for water and minerals. The time it takes for germination depends on the kind of seed, the warmth of the surrounding air and the amount of water available.

Extension
Chart growth rate by days for the seeds germinating in your classroom. You will show some variations but also show how predictable germination can be. This would be most appropriate in areas where farming occurs.

Science Notes
Such a simple activity but one that shows clearly the marvelous workings of living things. The process of germination is directed by messages contained in the plant DNA. Unless the proper conditions exist, germination does not begin and the seed can remain dormant (without activity) for ages. This activity can be done in plastic bags or jars. You can use soil or cotton to hold the moisture. The understanding of germination was an important step for mankind.

56. What Do the Birdies Eat? Tweet, Tweet!

Outcome
Students will germinate birdseed to understand that many varieties of plants provide food for birds.

Materials
For each student or group of students:
- commercial birdseed
- potting soil
- hand lens
- plastic, wide-mouth glasses
- water
- paper and pencil

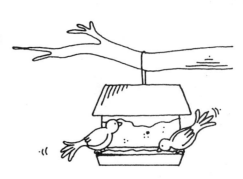

Engage Activity
Several days before this activity, set up a small bird-feeding station on the school grounds. Have students observe birds feeding. Ask children how they think birds would get food in nature.

Experimenting/Observing
Put potting soil in glass and water thoroughly. Sparsely sprinkle birdseed over the top of the soil. Gently press each seed into the soil. Put in sunny, warm area and water as needed (watch for overwatering!). Observe daily until plants have germinated and are several inches tall. Using hand lens as an aid, draw a sample of each different kind of plant in the glass. Compare plants between students.

Thinking
Did all the seeds look alike? Do all the plants that have germinated look alike? Why would birds eat seeds from different kinds of plants?

Explanation
Birds eat seeds from a variety of plants. The different-looking plants you germinated represent some of the many kinds of plants. Just as you eat different kinds of foods because that is what helps make you healthy, birds eat seeds from different kinds of plants. Different plants produce seeds at different times so that there is usually something for the birds to eat!

Extension
You can transplant the seedlings and continue to let them grow. Most will be grasses. You might want to study the beaks of seed-eating birds to see how they are adapted. This activity could lead to an exploration of different birds and their diets—from seeds to insects to fruits.

Science Notes
Not only does the variety of seeds eaten ensure a steady supply of seeds, it also provides insurance against a particular variety being wiped out by disease or mankind. The ecology of our planet provides habitats where the needs of all living things are met. It includes plant seeds for birds and bird fertilizer for plants!

57. Seeds Hiding in Fruit

Outcome
Students will understand that fruits cover and protect the seeds of plants.

Materials
For entire class:
- fruit samples such as strawberries, melons, peaches, peas in pods, tomatoes, apples, bananas, walnuts in shells, plums, oranges, cherries, grapes, wheat (can be purchased in hobby shops) or any other seeded fruit you can obtain

For each student:
- paper toweling
- hand lens
- plastic, serrated knife
- drawing paper and pencils

Engage Activity
Display fruit. Generate list of what all these fruits have in common. Ask for explanations of why you have included peas, tomatoes, wheat, nuts or grain in this exploration of fruits. Tell students that they are going on a seed hunt and that the seeds are hiding in the fruit.

Experimenting/Observing
Find the seed or seeds hidden in your fruit samples. Use serrated knife to cut into fruit if you need to. Use the hand lens to look for or to look at small seeds. Draw your observations. Include the seed and some of the fruit that was hiding the seed.

Thinking
Were any of your seeds hard to find? What covered and protected the seeds? What things did all of the seeds have in common? What things did all of the "fruits" have in common?

Explanation
Some seeds are large and easy to see and find. Others are small and easier to feel when you eat it than to see (raspberry). Fruit covers the seeds of plants. Most seeds have a hard covering and many of them have dark coloring. Most fruits have a fleshy part to them that is used for food by animals of all kinds. Fruits are the containers for seeds of a plant. Some fruits we think of as vegetables because they are not sweet. Although some vegetables, nuts and grains are really fruit, we don't usually call them fruit—but now you know the real secret!

Extensions
Investigate how edible fruits help disperse seeds. Crack open a coconut to see one of the largest seeds in nature!

Science Notes
A fruit is a highly developed ovary. How the various layers of ovary develop determines the type of fruit.

58. Mini Terrariums

Outcome
Students will build a self-contained botanical system.

Materials
For each student or group of students:
- 2 20-ounce (591-ml) clear, soft plastic glasses (remove the rim of one so that it fits snugly when placed upside down on the second glass)
- gravel (should be rock fragments no larger than ¾" (1.91 cm))
- potting soil (or good quality soil from your area)
- seedlings (can be purchased from plant nurseries or students can germinate them from the preceding activity)
- water
- florist's moss

Engage Activity
Complete activity "Wonderful Water to the Rescue" on page 53. Discuss the needs of plants. Have materials for this activity on display. Ask students to guess what you will be doing in this activity.

Experimenting/Observing
Have students label the uncut glasses with their names. Put 1" (2.54 cm) gravel on bottom of uncut glass. Put 1" (2.54 cm) soil on top of the gravel. Wet the soil lightly with water and tamp down with fingers. Poke holes in the soil where you want to plant. Gently place seedling in hole and firm soil around it. Place moss on top of soil and water until soil is wet. Firmly put cover over planted glass. Set in warm, sunny place and observe daily.

soil
gravel
moss

Thinking
What do plants need to grow? What have you given your plant so that it can grow? What do you think will happen to your plant? Will you need to water your plant? Will you need to give it fresh air?

Explanation
Plants need sunlight, warmth, water and nutrition from soil to grow. You have provided your plant with all these things. Because the leaves give off water vapor during the day it can be caught by the top of your terrarium as drops and fall back to the soil so you do not need to water the plant. Your plant also provides itself with oxygen during the same process.

Extension
You can keep track of plant growth by marking the outside of the plastic glass with a marker. Vary conditions of the terrarium: no light, no water, cold temperature, etc.

Science Notes
Green plants are able to cycle water, carbon dioxide and oxygen. Earth is a great big terrarium! The animal world is dependent on plants—without them there would be no life on Earth. Trees produce so much of the oxygen we need that the destruction of forests endangers the delicate balance we now enjoy.

59. Plant Parts

Outcome
Students will see plant parts and their diversity.

Materials
For entire class:
* plant specimens (houseplants; grass; small shrubs in containers; crop plants like corn, wheat, carrots and beans)
* while students watch, remove soils from around the roots of the plants

For each student or group of students:
* hand lens
* drawing paper and colored pencils

Engage Activity
Begin this activity with a walk through an area that has a variety of plants to observe (neighborhood, park, florist). Encourage students to describe what they observe.

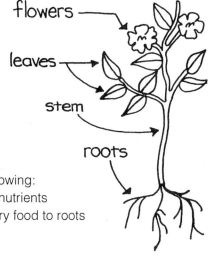

Experimenting/Observing
Draw a simple plant on the board and label the following:
    Roots—underground anchor, absorb water and nutrients
    Stems—support plant, carry water to leaves, carry food to roots
    Leaves—manufacture food
    Flowers—carry on reproduction

Have students observe parts of each plant with hand lens. Compare and contrast the parts of one plant with the others that they have examined. Draw three examples of different leaves you have seen. Draw two examples of stems you have seen. Draw two examples of roots you have seen. Draw two examples of flowers you have seen.

Thinking
Did you find all the parts of the plant in each example? Did all the leaves of all the plants look exactly alike? The stems? The roots? The flowers? Can you describe what it was that was different about each plant? Here are some words that can help: *rough, smooth, green, brown, jagged, round, long, short, woody, soft.*

Explanation
The members of the plant kingdom are as varied as members of the animal kingdom. Scientists and gardeners use the differences you have seen in roots, stems, leaves and flowers to help them identify plants. There are some plants that are so simple they do not have roots, stems or leaves—like pond scum!

Extension
Add information about the plants you provide according to the level of your students. You may want to include herbaceous, woody, annual, perennial, etc.

Science Notes
This activity looks at the more complex members of the plant kingdom, the vascular plants. They have specialized internal tubes that transport water and manufactured food throughout the plant. They also incorporate fibrous materials into the tissues which give these plants the ability to grow upright and therefore place their leaves in advantageous positions for gathering sunlight. From herbaceous pansies to woody redwood trees, these are the familiar plants of our lives that provide us food, shelter and natural beauty.

60. Inside Out a Flower

Outcome
Students will observe the anatomy of a flower.

Materials
For each student or group of students:
- tulip (This is the easiest flower to observe all its parts. Florists can provide flowers beyond their prime.)
- hand lens
- drawing paper and colored pencils
- piece of white paper
- plastic knives

Engage Activity
Let students make a list of everything they know about flowers. Introduce a simple vocabulary that will help them identify the parts of a flower:

Carpel—female part of the flower, found in the center

Stamens—male part of the flower, on stalks surrounding the carpel

Petals—the white or colored structures that surround the carpel and the stamens

Sepals—the leaf-like structures that cover a flower bud

Anther—the male part of the flower, produces pollen

Experimenting/Observing
Remove the petals from half of your flower so that you can see the inside of the flower more easily. Identify the parts of your flower. Inside out! Draw what you have observed. Cut off an anther and shake it on the white paper. Cut the carpel out of the flower. Cut it lengthwise.

Thinking
Did you find all the parts of the flower? Did anything shake out of the anther? What did you see when you cut into the carpel? What part do you think will form seeds for the next generation of flower plants?

Explanation
A flower is the reproductive part of a plant. Flowers make seeds which become the seedlings of the next generation. Anthers are the male part of the flower and produce pollen (the fine powder that shakes off on the white paper). The carpel is the female part of the flower and will produce the seeds. They are the tiny white things in the bottom of the carpel.

Extension
This activity is for the beginning science student. To this activity you can add vocabulary, inquiries into the reason for attractive petals, comparisons of shape of ovaries and the number of seeds that they contain.

Science Notes
Pollen from the stamens must reach the top of the carpel for fertilization of seeds to take place. Plants rely on insect feet to do this. The top of the carpel is sticky-sweet. Insects come for the nectar and leave pollen they have brushed up against. Colorful flowers attract the insects as does aroma.

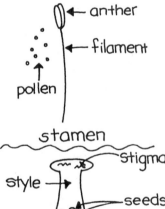

61. A Leaf Mosaic

Outcome
Students will observe the great diversity of leaf type, leaf textures, leaf sizes and leaf edges found in nature.

Materials
For the classroom:
- leaves—green and fresh (Gather as many different leaf types as you can to be passed around among students. Use houseplants, vegetables, shrubs, trees and grasses.)

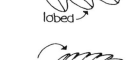

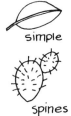

For each student or group of students:
- hand lens
- white glue
- white paper
- toothpick (a glue paintbrush)

Engage Activity
Have students look through the books available in your classroom to see how many different kinds of leaves are in the illustrations. Visit a place where they can see many different kinds of plants (park, neighborhood, florist).

Experimenting/Observing
Using your hand lens and your sense of touch, examine leaves. Make a mosaic of leaves on the white paper by painting the back of each leaf with glue. Include leaves that are different sizes, colors, textures, edges and shapes!

Thinking
Were all your leaves the same color of green? How many different shapes did you see? Count how many different edges there were in your leaf samples. Did all of the leaf samples feel the same? Did you feel a very smooth one? How about a scratchy one (grass rubbed the wrong way)? What difference was there in the sizes of different leaves? Are all plant leaves alike?

Explanation
Plant leaves have as much variety as animals' legs, or fins or wings. We identify plants by looking at their leaves. Leaves can be hairy, sticky or smooth. They can be large or very tiny. They can have straight edges or edges like a bread knife or curvy edges. They can be long and skinny, short and wide, or have many lobes. Their diversity is part of the wonderment of the natural world.

Extension
Students can study the arrangement of leaves on a stem or how the veins are arranged in the leaf.

Science Notes
Leaf edges are entire, serrated or lobed. Leaf texture is for protection, shedding water or catching rides on passing animals. Leaves are either simple (one to a leaf stalk) or compound (many leaflets growing from a single leaf stalk). Spines of cactus and tendrils of peas are specialized leaves.

62. From Plant Parts to Veggies

Outcome
Students will discover how common vegetables come from various plant parts.

Materials
- samples of the following vegetables for each student or group of students:
  - Leaves—cabbage, lettuce, spinach, Brussels sprouts
  - Bulbs—Spanish onion, green onion, garlic
  - Tubers—potatoes (both sweet and regular)
  - Roots—carrot, radish, beets, turnip
  - Stalks—rhubarb, asparagus, celery
- paper toweling
- drawing paper and pencils
- plastic, serrated knife
- hand lens

tuber vegetables

leaf vegetables

cabbage

potato

Engage Activity
Review with students the parts of a plant. Add to this list bulbs (daffodil bulb—thick pad of stem with white fleshy leaves surrounding it) and tubers (potato—stem that is found underground and is swollen with stored food).

root vege-tables

Experimenting/Observing
Observe your supply of vegetables. Compare and contrast them with each other. Use the hand lens to help you. Divide vegetables into groups of leaves, bulbs, tubers, roots and stalks. Use knife to find the short, fat stem of the bulbs. Record your findings by drawing an example of each plant part you have seen.

carrot

bulb vege-tables

Thinking
What do you see that surprises you? Which vegetables are made of leaves? Of bulbs? Of tubers? Of roots? Of stalks? Do you think your next trip to the grocery store's produce section might be more interesting?

onion

stalk vegetables

Science Notes
The primary source of energy on Earth is the sun. Plants are able to turn that energy into stored food. When we eat plant parts, that energy then is available to us. As animals, we are not able to make our own food (stored energy).

Explanation
Leafy vegetables include cabbage, endive, Chinese cabbage, spinach, Brussels sprouts and lettuce. Bulbs include onions, garlic, leek and shallots. Tubers include potatoes, sweet potatoes and Jerusalem artichokes. Roots include carrots, radishes, beets, turnips, parsnips and rutabagas. Stalk vegetables include rhubarb, asparagus and celery. The nutrition from vegetables is made by leaves and stored in various places.

Extension
Combine fruits and vegetables for a tasting experience. Describe differences in taste between all these plant parts that we eat.

asparagus

63. How Does a Garden Grow?

Outcome
Students will learn of three things necessary for healthy plant growth.

Materials
For each student or group of students:
- 4 seedlings (can germinate bean seeds)
- 4 Styrofoam™ coffee cups
- plastic glass (with ounce [ml] increments marked on side)
- ruler, paper, pencil
- potting soil
- small-sized gravel

Have ready for classroom use:
- picnic coolers (keep lid open)
- daily supply of ice (or cold packs to keep low temperature)

Engage Activity
Have students generate a list of those things they need to grow up healthy. Next to that list, have students generate a list of things they think that a plant may need to grow up healthy. Explain that they will be doing a scientific experiment to see how important light, water and warmth are to growing plants.

Experimenting/Observing
Place ½" (1.27 cm) gravel in bottom of cup and 1½" (3.81 cm) soil above that. Plant seedlings in soil. Water seedlings with 2 ounces (60 ml) of water. Mark cups A, B, C and D. Put cups A and C in a warm, sunlit spot. Put cup B under an opened lunch sack in a warm spot. Place cup D in picnic cooler. Water cups A, B and D with 2 ounces (60 ml) of water every other day. Water cup C with 1 ounce (30 ml) of water every other day. Measure growth of each plant with ruler once a week. Record data for each plant on paper. Continue for one month. (Teacher note: Increase or decrease amount of watering according to the soil used and humidity in your area.)

Thinking
Which plant appears to be growing up healthy? If one or more of your plants is not growing successfully, can you explain why not? What important thing for good plant growth was kept from plant B? Plant C? Plant D? What do you think would eventually happen to each plant?

Explanation
Light, water and warmth are important to growing plants. If they are not provided in sufficient supply, the growth of the plant would not be all that it could be.

Extension
Growth rates can be graphed. Other criteria besides height can be used: number of secondary leaves, intensity of color or strength of stems.

Science Notes
Temperature, water and sunlight exposure are crucial ingredients for successful seed germination. Springtime with its warmer temperatures and prolonged hours of sunlight facilitates the beginning of the life cycle of plants. Soil moisture from winter snows and seasonal spring rains provide another key ingredient. Drought and floods disrupt the availability and balance of temperature, sunlight and water. Greenhouses provide an eternal spring environment!

64. Plant Signs of Spring

Outcome
Students will become aware of the changes that take place in the plant world as plants come out of dormancy.

Materials
For classroom:
- large chart where signs of spring may be recorded

For each student or group of students:
- examples of grass turning green, tree branch where green is present when scraped with fingernail, twigs or branches that have leaf or flower buds on them, examples of early flowers (tulips, crocus, grape hyacinths)
- hand lens
- plastic, serrated knife
- drawing paper and pencils

Engage Activity
Discuss the kinds of clothes that your students might wear during the winter and during the summer. Ask why they wear different things during different seasons. Discuss what plants might do to keep themselves safe from the winter cold. Discuss what plants can do once spring comes.

Experimenting/Observing
Carefully observe each thing your teacher has provided. Use your hand lens for a closer look at things. Use your knife if you want to look inside a plant part. Scrape a patch out of the outer layer of your twigs. Record those things that are different from a winter plant by drawing them.

Thinking
What parts of the plants are the same as they are in the winter? What parts are different than they are in the winter? Why is it safe for plants to have flowers and leaves at this time of the year?

Explanation
Woody plants still have twigs and branches during the winter. Their leaves are gone, otherwise they would freeze during the cold temperatures of winter. There are still blades of grass during the winter. In the spring, the plant knows that the temperature will be warm and that it will be safe to grow leaves and flowers. The appearance of both leaves and flowers signals the end of winter and the beginning of spring.

Extension
Look into signs of spring in the animal world—worms in the soil, birds returning and building nests, etc.

Science Notes
Plants become dormant during winter in order to minimize the risk of freezing. Spring temperatures and increased hours of light stimulate plants to produce leaves and reproduce.

65. Bird Feeding in Winter

Outcome
Students will make a bird feeder filled with a mixture that is healthy for birds during the winter.

Materials
For each student or group of students:
- pinecone
- peanut butter
- margarine tubs (or equivalent)
- commercial birdseed mix (amount will depend on size of pinecones)
- twine (about 18" [45.72 cm] lengths)
- wooden craft sticks

Engage Activity
This is a wintertime activity. Have students tally the number of birds they see around school and home for a week's duration. Discuss what these birds are eating and where they are getting their food.

Experimenting/Observing
Mix birdseed and peanut butter with wooden stick in tub. Using wooden stick as a tool, place the birdseed mixture inside the pinecone. Tamp it down so it is secure. Tie one end of the twine around the pinecone. Tie other end of twine to a branch of a tree.

Thinking
What is the difference in temperature between summer and winter? Why do you think you have added peanut butter to the birdseed? What part of the bird will help it reach inside the pinecone for the goodies you have put there? Why do we hang bird feeders from trees? Why should we feed the birds in the winter? Do you need to feed the birds in the summer?

Explanation
In the winter the cold temperatures mean that birds use up more calories to keep warm. Peanut butter and the fat that it contains give the birds a concentrated source of calories that they can use to keep warm. Bird beaks are shaped so that birds can reach into all sorts of places to get food. Birds use trees for places to build their nests and as resting places. When we put the bird feeders there, they have a good chance of seeing them. Because our houses and buildings take up room that used to grow plants with seeds, we need to make up for the lost plants by feeding the birds. In the summer there is usually enough food for all birds because they can eat things besides seeds.

Extension
Follow up this activity with some serious bird-watching. Observe how birds fly. Identify common birds of your area. Study bird size and temperament at feeding sites.

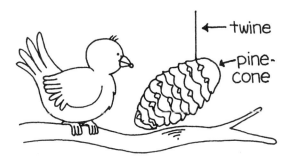

← twine

←pine-
cone

Science Notes
Bird-watching is a cheap, satisfying hobby for people of all ages. As bird populations decrease in urban areas, it is essential to feed them if you are to enjoy them!

66. Super Swimmers—Fish!

Outcome
Students will observe the ways that fish move through the water and be able to identify the fins responsible.

Materials
- You will need to borrow at least one goldfish in an aquarium. Your students will need time for their observations so you need to have your "subject" in the classroom and provide plenty of time for individual observations.

caudal fin
(side to side)

dorsal fin
(balance)

ventral fin

pelvic fins

pectoral fins
(forward and backward)

Engage Activity
Have students generate a list of body parts used by various animals for movement. Influence discussion to include wiggling animals (worms, snakes), flying animals (birds, bats), animals with legs (horses, man) and swimming animals (fish, whales). Have students make predictions about how fish move.

Experimenting/Observing
Count the number of fins on the fish you are going to study. Watch the fish swim for a while until you can describe all the different ways your fish is able to move. Watch the fins closely as the fish swims forward and backward and decide which fin is responsible for this. Watch the fins closely and decide which fins are responsible for helping the fish keep its balance. Draw a picture of your fish and its fins.

Thinking
How many fins did you see on your fish? Can you describe or imitate the movements a fish can make? Where are the fins located that are responsible for moving the fish forward and backward? Where is the fin that moves the fish from side to side? Where are the fins that help balance the fish? Can your fish move quickly? How do you think that will help the fish stay alive in the natural world?

Explanation
Your goldfish has seven fins. Four of these (2 pairs) are toward the bottom of the fish where you might expect to find legs on a land animal. These help the fish move up and down, forward and backward. The large fin that is the tail of the fish pushes the fish through the water and steers it from side to side. The fin on top of the fish helps balance the fish and works when the fish changes direction. Fish move quickly to catch dinner or to avoid being dinner!

Extension
Dissect a cooked fish to show bone structure of the pectoral and pelvic fins. Compare the structure of a fish to the structure of a canoe with its paddles.

Science Notes
The wondrous movements of fish through water are a result of skeletal adaptations that result in fins. These fins are strong and flexible because of the slender bones and large muscles that are attached to them. Fish bodies are shaped for ease of movement through water. Fish and fin shapes have been widely copied by mankind in an attempt to move through water more easily.

67. Mighty, Marvelous, Marching Ants

Outcome
Students will observe how ants find food, convey information to other ants and carry food back to their homes.

Materials
This is an outdoor activity which requires an anthill. Preview the area for any hazards.

For each student or group of students:
- sheet of white paper
- supply of bread crumbs
- supply of fruit pieces (use fragrant fruit such as apples)
- felt-tip marker
- hand lens

Engage Activity
Lead a discussion of experiences your students have had with ants or observations they have made.

Experimenting/Observing
Position students about 10 feet (3.05 m) from anthill and allow 6 feet (1.83 m) between groups of students. Place paper on ground with pieces of fruit and several pieces of bread on the paper. Wait for ants to discover the food. When food is discovered, carefully observe the path that the ants take to find the food and to carry it away. Mark the path with your marker. Put pieces of fruit and bread in another position on the paper. Observe the new path that the ants take. Mark that path. Count the number of ants needed to move a piece of fruit. Place some soil directly on the path that the ants are using. Observe their actions.

Thinking
How do you think the ants found the food you had for them? Did ants begin to follow a path to the food? What happened when you moved the food? What happened when you put soil on the path? What do ants do when a piece of food is too heavy for one ant? Were you surprised at how much they could carry? How is the ant world like our world?

Explanation
Ants use a sense of smell to find food. They leave a scent trail for the other ants to follow so they can help with the job of supplying food to their community. Ants will follow an old trail after you move the food source because that scent trail is still there. When you block the path with soil it takes a while for the ants to pick up the scent trail again. Ants can carry an amazing amount of weight compared to their body weight. They use cooperation to bring food back to their community just as farmers and truckers cooperate to bring us food.

Science Notes
As successive ants follow the scent trail to food, the trail becomes less tortuous. They soon develop a relatively straight path. In some ant species only the larvae (immature stage) can digest solid food and provide liquid food for the rest of the colony. The worker ants we observe are responsible for finding and transporting solid food back to the larvae. Some ant species keep aphids handy to "milk"; others appear to "farm" fungus for food. From small black ants to fierce army ants, this group of insects is the most numerous on Earth.

68. Spiderweb Patterns

Outcome
Students will observe the intricate patterns in spiderwebs.

Materials
Fall is the best time for this activity. Students must be in an environment where spiderwebs are available and easily accessed. Give appropriate warnings about spiders.

For each student or group of students:
- talcum powder
- drawing paper and pencils

Engage Activity
Read a story about spiders. Have students generate a list of what they know about spiders.

Experimenting/Observing
Locate a spiderweb. Put a small amount of talcum powder in the palm of your hand. Very gently blow the powder into the spiderweb until the strands are white and easy to see. Observe the pattern of your spiderweb. Draw what you see.

start

web in progress

finished → web

Thinking
Why did you need to put talcum powder on the spider's web? What did your spider use to anchor its web? Could you see a pattern to your spider's web? Did you see the spider that made the web? Why do spiders build webs?

Explanation
The material that spiders use to weave their webs is hard to see. Spiders do not want their webs to be seen so that it is easier to catch their prey. The talcum powder made the web easy for you to see. Spiders anchor their webs on surrounding tree branches, other plant parts or man-made materials like fence posts or walls. Spiders usually use something that won't move when the wind blows or collapse when the web has something in it. Spiders weave their webs in patterns that are very exact, particularly if they find anchors that are positioned in a square or rectangle. The spider is usually not very far away from its web. Sometimes they hang from a thread of the web itself. Spiderwebs are actually insect traps. Spiders eat what they catch in their webs.

Extension
Spread glue from a large glue stick on an oversized piece of black paper. Slowly and carefully move the paper in back of the web and bring it through the web, catching the web on paper without disturbing the pattern.

Science Notes
Not all spiders spin webs to catch their prey. Some are hunters that chase their prey. Spiders have two body parts, eight legs and two pairs of specialized appendages near their mouths. The tip of the abdomen contains three pairs of spinnerets that exude material to build webs, cocoons and egg sacs.

69. Stuffed Animal Parade

Outcome

Students will use their stuffed animals as models to observe certain physical characteristics of animals.

Materials

For classroom to share:

- stuffed animals that students have brought from home
- adhesive-backed name tag for each animal containing owner's name
- teacher-supplied photographs of animals mounted on cardboard

Engage Activity

Tell students that you need to determine if all the stuffed toys and photographs are really animals. Discuss the following criteria and eliminate any toys or photos that are not animals: Are capable of independent movement, feelings and sensations. Do not have body parts of wood or parts that are green and can manufacture food.

Experimenting/Observing

Have students work in groups. Look at all the animals in your group very carefully. Share what you see and think about what you see with your group. Divide your animals into groups using the following reasons. (Try to figure out what difference these things will mean in the life of your animals.)

size in real life	length of legs
where they live	type of feet
how they move	length of tail
which make good pets	their coats (hair, feather, scales)

Thinking

Does each animal belong to many different groups? How would being a large animal help the animal? What kinds of movements could your animals make? What can feet tell you about an animal? Why does an animal have a tail? What does an animal's coat tell you about where it lives?

Explanation

Animals have many characteristics and will belong to many groups. Scientists use groupings so that animals in a group are very much like each other. A large animal usually doesn't have as many enemies as small ones. Animals can walk with legs, fly with wings and swim with fins. But, animals with legs can swim if they have to and not all birds have wings. Animals' feet can tell you if they use them to dig and what kind of ground they live on (camels with big feet for sand, deer with tiny feet for rocky soil). Animals use tails for balance, to fight, to hang onto branches or to swat away annoying insects. An animal's coat tells scientists what large group of animals it belongs to (hair—mammals, feathers—birds, scales—fish). Many animals would not make good pets. Dogs and cats are the most common pets.

Science Notes

The physical characteristics of an animal give us many clues to its behavior, environment and ultimately its identification. Animal groupings can include predators, grazers, arctic or jungle dwellers, nighttime hunters, tree climbers, swift runners or those with incredible senses of smell, hearing or sight.

As students become more sophisticated about the animal world, they will recognize more characteristics and be able to describe their significance.

70. Eye Clues

Outcome
Students will be able to determine if an animal is a predator or prey by the position of its eyes.

Materials
Use materials from "Stuffed Animal Parade" activity on page 69. Pictures of animal faces mounted on cardboard will be particularly helpful in this activity. Provide paper and pencils for drawing results or word descriptions.

Experimenting/Observing
Using your own eyes, decide how far to the side you can see without moving your head. How much can you see in front? Pretend your eyes are on the side of your head. Try to decide what you will be able to see without moving your head. Divide your stuffed animals and your animal pictures into two groups:
  animals with eyes in the front of their faces
  animals with eyes on the side of their faces
Label one piece of paper "PREDATOR" and another "PREY." Draw or describe animals with eyes in front on the first page. On the second page, draw or describe animals with eyes on the side.

Thinking
Which eye position would be best for an animal that hunted for its food? Why? Which eye position would be best for an animal that had to continually watch out for enemies that wanted to eat it? Why? Which animals are predators? Which animals are prey? What are human beings? What must we do if a tiger is trying to catch us for its dinner? Does man have many natural enemies that normally try to eat people?

Explanation
Animals that hunt for their food need to be able to see clearly the animal that they are chasing. When their eyes are in the front of their faces they can see things in front or slightly to the side with ease. These are called "predators." Animals that are often chased need to be able to see behind them without having to turn their heads. Having eyes on the side of their faces helps them. These animals are called "prey." Humans are most often predators. Our eyes are located in the front, and we must turn our heads to see what is behind us. When we do this and run at the same time it is easy to lose our balance and slow down or fall.

Extension
Further explore the role of vision in hunting by covering one eye as you catch a ball. Two eyes give us more information than just one eye!

Science Notes
Eye position is an example of adaptation in nature. The head start given to prey by being able to spot their enemies as soon as they come into view can mean the difference between life and death. This is an easily recognized adaptation.

71. A Penny for Your Drops

Outcome
Students will understand the concept of surface tension.

Materials
For each student:
- 2 or 3 sheets of absorbent paper toweling
- 1 penny (washed in vinegar and salt, rinsed, dried)
- 1 dropper (the inexpensive, all-plastic type is fine)
- 1 small container of water
- tin can lid
- piece of metal screen
- needle
- spoon

Engage Activity
Have a clear container of water ready to demonstrate surface tension for the students. Slip a needle from a spoon onto the water, carefully place a piece of metal screen, and a tin can lid, on top of the water. Let students observe the object closely, from the top and the sides. Then push each item to the bottom of your container to show that it was not "floating" because it was less dense than the water.

Experimenting/Observing
Have students carefully place one drop after another of water on top of the penny until it "spills."

Have students observe and describe what they see happening to the shape of the water on top of the penny.

If appropriate, have student count the number of drops the penny will hold for each try.

Thinking
What happened that surprised you? What did the penny look like when it had many drops on it? How many drops would your penny hold? What do you think is holding the water together on top of the penny? What do you have on the surface of your body that holds everything in?

Explanation
Water has a "skin" that helps it stick together on the surface. This is called "surface tension."

Extension
You may want the students to compare and contrast doing this activity with heads or tails, hot or cold water.

Science Notes:
Water molecules have a slight polarity, i.e. a negative and a positive end. The attraction between the negative and positive ends of surrounding molecules help keep them tightly bound. The topmost molecules have only the molecules underneath them to bind to. This leads to such a strong bond it seems like a skin. The insect water skipper (water bug, pond skater) takes advantage of surface tension and it is able to walk on water. We too could do this if our legs were far enough apart and our feet were very large!

72. To Float or to Sink

Outcome
Students will understand that some matter will sink in water and other will float in water.

Materials
- clear container of water (large enough to hold two cans of Pepsi™)
- cork
- nail
- piece of wood
- toothpicks
- modeling clay
- 1 can of Pepsi™, 1 can of Diet Pepsi™

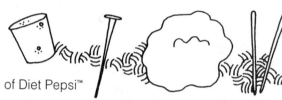

Engage Activity
Have a large, clear container of water and items that students can predict whether they will sink or float (marbles, paper, etc.). Get a consensus of opinion from the students and then place each item in the water. Next put a can of regular Pepsi™ and a can of Diet Pepsi™ in the water. Leave them during the rest of the activity.

Experimenting/Observing
Have students see which things will float and which will sink. Using the toothpick and clay, place a small amount of clay on the toothpick and return it to the water. Keep increasing/decreasing the size of clay around other toothpicks.

Thinking
Which things floated in the water? Which things sank in water? What amount of clay allowed the toothpick to float? To sink? What is the difference between the Pepsi™ and the Diet Pepsi™ that could cause one to sink and one to float?

Explanation
We can describe some matter by telling whether it will sink or float in water. If it is heavier than water, it will sink. If it is lighter than water, it will float. The liquid in regular Pepsi™ is heavier because it has a lot of sugar. The Diet Pepsi™ liquid has a small amount of artificial sweetener rather than the heavy sugar.

Extension
This activity can be extended by testing many other items. Children should become confident in predicting what will float and what will sink. If you use things like toy boats, rubber ducks, etc., you will be entering into the realm of buoyancy and must emphasize that these items are made of material plus air spaces.

Science Notes
The can of regular Pepsi™ has sugar in it. The Diet Pepsi™ has NutraSweet™. 1 teaspoon (5 ml) Nutrasweet™ = 12 teaspoons (60 ml) sugar. The regular Pepsi™ is therefore heavier!

The density of a substance determines whether it will sink or float in another substance. Density, or how heavy something is for its size, pertains to matter in all its states. Solids can float in liquids (wood in water), liquids can float in liquids (oil and water), gases can float in liquids (carbonation in soda pop). Gases can float or sink in gases (helium balloons in air). The numerical density values of substances are based on water as being 1. A density of 2 means something is twice as dense as water.

73. Floating Bottles

Outcome
Students will understand that air is lighter than water. They will understand why a container filled with air can float.

Materials

For group of students:
- bucket, tub or other deep container of water
- empty, clean plastic salad dressing bottles that have narrow necks
- plastic tubing for each student (length determined by your water container)
- various floating toys

Engage Activity
Have a tub of water with rubber duck, toy boats and other floating toys in it. Let students manipulate the objects for a time.

Experimenting/Observing
Have bottle already sunk at the bottom of the container. Give students pieces of tubing. Tell them to raise the bottle using the tubing and air from their lungs. Let them sink and refloat the bottles as many times as needed until the association between air and water has been made.

Thinking
Why does something sink? Why did the bottle sink? What did you see coming to the surface as the salad bottle sank? Why does something float? What did you do to the salad bottle so that it could float? Why do rubber duckies float? Why do boats float?

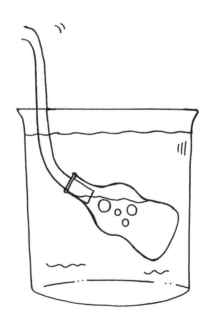

Explanation
When things are heavier than water, they will sink. The salad dressing bottle filled with water is heavier than water, therefore it will sink. Things that are lighter than water will float. When you blew air into the bottle, you made it full of air rather than water. Air is lighter than water, so the bottle plus the air in it was lighter than water and it floated.

Extension
The next activity in this book is the next step of understanding floating and sinking, or *buoyancy*.

Science Notes
Density is the amount of matter compared to size, or how heavy something is for its size. The replacement of water with air changes the density of the bottle. The density of the bottle and its contents are considered as a whole — just as a boat is the sum of its shell, cargo and air spaces. When that whole is less dense than water, the object will float. When that whole is more dense than water, the object will sink.

74. Boat Float

Outcome
Students will have an understanding of how boats float in water.

Materials
- large container(s) for water—wide, not deep
- toys made for floating (include one boat that you can add cargo to)
- modeling clay
- paper toweling

Engage Activity
Silently, add each floating toy to the water. Take clay balls (cargo) and add, one at a time, to the boat until it sinks.

Experimenting/Observing
Supply each student with modeling clay. Ask students to make boats that will float and will hold cargo. Encourage them to test their designs often. They can pluck the "sinkers" out, dry them off and modify their designs. When they have a boat that floats, they can start adding cargo (small clay balls). They can keep refining their designs as time allows. You may want to set this up as an activity center for several days.

Thinking
Does clay usually sink in water? What did you have to do to the clay to make it float? Why did some boats sink? Why did some boats float? Why is it important that boats hold cargo?

Explanation
Boats are made of materials that are heavier than water and would sink if they were not in a boat shape. Boats that float do so because they hold a lot of air. When the weight of a boat plus the air it holds is less than the weight of water, it will float. Boats are used to carry people and all the things they need. You cannot put too much cargo into a boat or it will become heavier than water and sink.

Extension
If you give each student the same quantity of clay, you can compare designs and carrying capacity. You could have students figure the Plimsol line on their boats—how low in the water it can float before sinking with the addition of more cargo.

Science Notes
Archimedes was the first to figure out that buoyancy depended on the weight of an object versus the weight of the water it displaces (pushes away). When that weight is less than water, the structure will float. Although made of materials that are heavier than water, a boat is designed with many air spaces so that its total weight is less than the weight of the water it will displace. Large ships are surprisingly hollow when you look at them in cross section—so much so that they can hold tons of cargo and still be buoyant in water!

75. Let's Go to the North Pole!

Outcome
Students will understand the connection between magnets and compasses. They will use a compass to find directions to the earth's magnetic north pole.

Materials
- 2 bar magnets for each student
- 1 compass for each student
- straight pins (Adult supervision is needed!)
- thread

Engage Activity
Have a display of compasses used by hikers and boaters. Magnetize straight pins by stroking them along a bar magnet. Hang them from the ceiling with thread so that they are parallel to the floor. They should all be oriented in a north-south position. Define *attract* and *repel*.

Experimenting/Observing
Put the ends of the magnets together in every possible combination. Describe what happens each time. Have students find North in your classroom with the compass. Put magnet next to compass. Describe what happens to the needle of the compass. For each magnet, label the end that repels the north end of the needle as North and the end that attracts the north end of the needle as South. Repeat first part of the activity.

Thinking
What does "attract" feel like? What does "repel" feel like? What end of the magnet repelled the north end of the compass needle? What do north ends of the magnet do—attract or repel? What do the south ends do—attract or repel? What happens between south and north ends—attraction or repulsion?

Science Notes
A compass needle is a bar magnet that floats free. You can make any magnet a compass by letting it "float" free on the end of a string. Magnetic stones have been used since ancient times as a navigational aid. Magnetic north pole is not at the same exact spot as the geographic north pole.

Explanation
Like poles repel, unlike poles attract. A compass uses the magnetic attraction of the earth's north pole to move the needle. When a magnet is held next to a compass, the compass will respond to the stronger magnet's forces instead of earth's forces. The north end of the needle will be attracted to the south end of the magnet and repelled by the north end of the magnet.

Extension
Using compass readings, give directions from your classroom to the cafeteria. Become familiar with all the directions on a compass: North, South, East, West, SSE, NNW, SE, etc.

76. Water, Water, Everywhere

Outcome
Students will see the properties of a liquid, measure the volume of liquids and see how a liquid seeks its own level.

Materials
- water with blue food coloring
- clear containers of various shapes (tall and skinny, short and fat glasses, flat plastic sandwich holder, clear bowls, etc.)
- liquid measuring cup (You can make your own with clear plastic cups and a felt-tip marker.)
- clear PVC tubing, large diameter, cut into 2' to 3' (.61 to .91 m) lengths

Engage Activity
Set up a colorful display of various shapes of glass or clear plastic containers each with the same amount of colored water in it. Ask children if they think that each container has the same amount of water in it. Tally the yes and no votes. Then pour the water from each container into a clear measuring container. Empty after each measurement. Pour water into several containers and hold them in front of a desk so that the top of the water is level with the top of the desk. Tilt the container—point out that the water remains level with the top of the container.

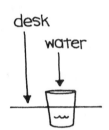

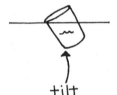

Experimenting/Observing
Let students measure the same amount of water each time they fill one of the containers you have provided. Let them empty and fill until they understand that the same amount of water can take any shape, i.e. tall and skinny can equal short and wide. Have them put the PVC tubing in a u-shape and pour water until it is about ⅓ full (you can predetermine this amount). The students can then hold it so that the water levels are even with their desktops. Have them manipulate the tubing by pulling up one side and then the other. The water will remain level with the desktop.

Science Notes
Liquids assume the shape of their containers because of the loose connection between molecules of a liquid. This also allows a liquid to flow. Glass is actually a very viscous liquid! Old windows will be thicker at the bottom—they are flowing downward very slowly!

Thinking
Does water have a definite shape? What can you do with water that you can't do with a solid? When water stays "level" does it remind you of something you would see in a carpenter's workshop?

Explanation
Water (or liquids) take the shape of their containers. You can pour water because it has no shape of its own. Water at the top of a container is level with the earth's surface. In this way it is like a carpenter's level.

Extension
Explore why water spreads out over a surface when it spills.

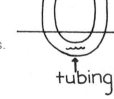

77. Fresh and Saltwater Eggs

Outcome
Students will experience the density difference between fresh water and salt water.

Materials
- water
- fresh eggs
- kosher salt
- craft sticks for stirring
- large, clear plastic glasses

Engage Activity
When the children arrive for class, have an egg floating in the middle of a large glass. You can even put a smiley face on the fresh egg with permanent markers. Fill the glass half-full with fresh water. Make a saltwater solution by stirring 4-6 tablespoons (60-90 ml) of salt into a half a glass of water. Using a funnel, slowly pour the salt water into the bottom of the glass. Place the egg in the glass. Quiz your students to see if they can explain what they are seeing.

Experimenting/Observing
Have students:

1. Fill both glasses with fresh water.
2. Put 8 tablespoons (120 ml) of salt into water of one glass.
3. Stir until salt is dissolved
4. Carefully place fresh egg in each glass.

Thinking
What happened to the egg in fresh water? What happened to the egg in the salt water? What is the difference between fresh water and salt water?

Explanation
Salt water is more dense than fresh water, so an egg will float in salt water because it weighs less than the water it displaces.

Extension
What difference will salt water make to boats? *(They float higher in the water.)* To swimmers? *(It's easier to float.)*

Science Notes
When salt is dissolved in water it becomes more dense, i.e. it has a greater mass to its volume. Ships will carry more cargo in salt water because they have more buoyancy in salt water. The Great Salt Lake has such a great salt content that it makes floating a breeze!

78. Candle, Candle, Burning Bright

Outcome
Students will see that fire needs oxygen to burn.

Materials
- tea light candles
- matches
- drinking glass (not plastic)

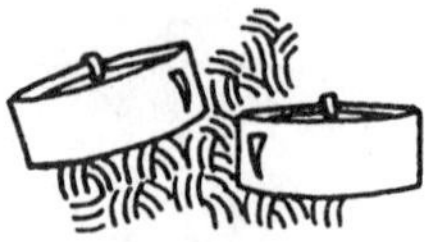

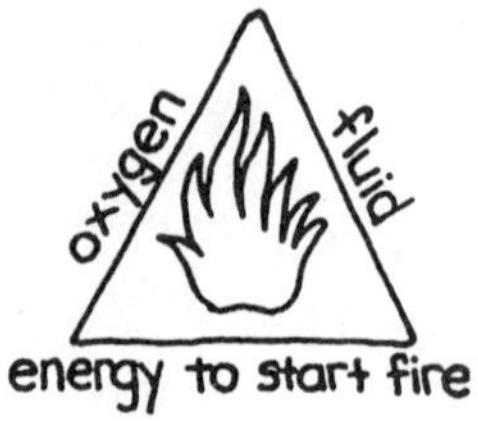

Engage Activity
Make a poster, or draw the diagram on the chalkboard for the Fire Triangle. Discuss with your students how each side of the triangle must be present for a fire to burn. Fire extinguishers and fire safety practices aim to eliminate one side of the triangle. Energy to start a fire can be matches, lightning or anything that brings fuel up to its combustion point.

Experiment/Observing
Be sure you are aware of the safety codes in your building or your district before you begin the activities involving candle flames. You may want to do this as a demonstration only or have some parents come in to be extra eyes and hands for this activity. If this is done in demonstration style, please go through it enough times so all students see and have made the connection you are looking for.

1. Light tea candle.
2. Put glass over burning candle.
3. Remove glass after flame has been out for awhile.

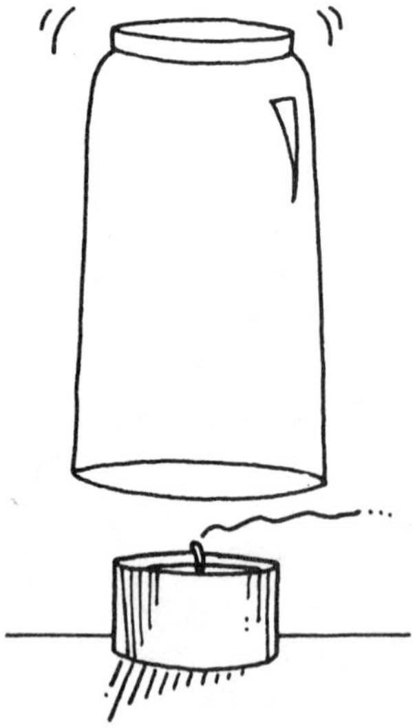

Thinking
What was the fuel side of the fire triangle in this experiment? Where was the oxygen for the oxygen side of the fire triangle? What supplied the energy to start the fire? Why did the fire go out? What side of the fire triangle did you eliminate to put out the fire? Why is a fire blanket like the glass?

Explanation
When the glass was placed over the candle it contained a certain amount of oxygen in its air. When that oxygen was used up in the fire, the fire stopped. The oxygen side of the fire triangle was eliminated.

Extension
Older students can experiment with lifting the glass off the candle in time to rekindle the flame although it appears the fire is out. The wick remains at a high enough temperature for a few seconds to provide the ignition energy.

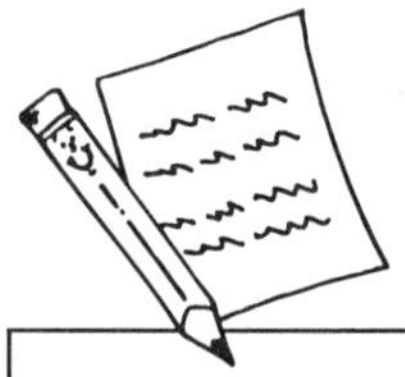

Science Notes
Fire is a natural curiosity to children. A thorough understanding of fire is knowledge that everyone should have. Emphasis can be placed on fire safety and prevention and brought into other aspects of your classroom during this discovery period. Questions about forest fires, controlled burns and the role of fire in ecology are most appropriately discussed at this point. Fire is a chemical reaction that releases energy in the form of heat, light and sound.

79. How Much Oxygen to Burn a Candle?

Outcome
Students will observe a way to see how much oxygen from the air is used to burn a candle for a short period of time.

Materials
- regular candles cut to fit glasses (see diagram)
- modeling clay
- bowl
- matches
- drinking glass (not plastic)
- water

Engage Activity
Review Fire Triangle. What things are needed for a fire to burn? Discuss that oxygen is found in air. Have students guess how much of air is oxygen.

Experimenting/Observing
This is best as a demonstration.

1. Secure candle in bowl with modeling clay.
2. Fill bowl with water so that bottom third of candle is underwater.
3. Put two pieces of clay on lip of glass across from one another.
4. Light candle and let it burn for a while.
5. Cover with glass resting on clay on bottom of bowl.
6. Measure the difference in the water level between the bowl and the glass with a permanent marker. Repeat two or three times.

Thinking
What happened to the flame after the glass was put over it? What happened to the level of the water in the glass? What happened to the level of the water in the bowl? Why did the level of the water in the glass rise while the level of the water in the bowl got lower?

Explanation
As the fire uses up the oxygen in the glass, water rushes in to replace it. So the water goes up in the glass and down in the bowl. The amount of water that went into the glass is the same as the amount of oxygen used up by the fire. Since air is about one fifth or 20% oxygen, the water rose about one fifth of the way up the glass.

Science Notes
As the oxygen is used up by the chemical reaction of fire, it is replaced by the water as if vacuumed up into the glass. Although the measurement is far from precise, it should be obvious to your students that a portion of air contains oxygen. Most students will be surprised to learn that oxygen is only 23% of air, nitrogen 75% and Argon 1%. The remaining gases in air are carbon dioxide, neon, helium, krypton, hydrogen, xenon and ozone. The current concerns about carbon dioxide and ozone buildup are because these gases threaten the mixture that has enabled life to flourish on Earth.

80. Homemade Fire Extinguisher

Outcome
Students will observe what happens in a fire reaction when air is replaced by carbon dioxide.

Materials
- 1-liter plastic soda bottles, emptied and clean
- vinegar and baking soda
- tea light candles and matches
- various fire extinguishers

Engage Activity
Have on display several fire extinguishers from your classroom, a home-size extinguisher, a fire blanket and anything you borrow from the local fire station. Have on display the Fire Triangle from the "Candle, Candle, Burning Bright" activity on page 78. Review the fire triangle. Emphasize that to fight a fire, one side of the triangle must be unavailable to the fire. Discuss how fire extinguishers, fire blankets and other fire-fighting equipment work to remove oxygen from the fire, thus putting it out.

Experimenting/Observing
This should be done as a demonstration.

1. Light tea light candle.
2. Pour 1 cup (240 ml) of vinegar into the soda bottle.
3. Slide a tablespoon (15 ml) of baking soda into the soda bottle (use a folded piece of paper).
4. Shake the contents with a swirling motion.
5. "Pour" the gas that has been produced over the flame. Be careful not to pour out the liquid, only the gas. It helps to hold the bottle almost parallel to the table you are working on. Repeat until you can do it quickly and smoothly. Contents of bottle can be disposed of down the sink.

Thinking
What happened when the vinegar and baking soda were mixed together? What happened when the gas produced was "poured" on the candle flame? How do you know that the gas produced was not oxygen? What side of the fire triangle was eliminated?

Explanation
Carbon dioxide is produced when baking soda and vinegar are mixed. Because carbon dioxide is heavier than air, it can be "poured" out of the bottle. When the carbon dioxide is poured over the flame, it replaces the oxygen from the air. Without oxygen the fire goes out.

Extension
Arrange several tea light candles or birthday candles on a slope and see how far down the carbon dioxide will flow.

Science Notes
Adding vinegar to baking soda results in a chemical reaction where the gas, carbon dioxide is produced. The carbon dioxide molecule is heavy enough to pour through air by pushing the air out of its way. Fire extinguishers all work on the principle that a fire must be deprived of oxygen. They also depend on chemical reactions that produce CO_2 or other compounds that will replace air.

81. Ups and Downs

Outcome

Students will observe floating and sinking of a solid in a liquid because of the addition of a gas (carbon dioxide).

Materials

- clear soda (Club soda is great because spills aren't sticky.)
- tall, plastic glasses
- raisins or popcorn (dry either on cookie sheet on low in oven)
- clear container of water
- various items (some that float)

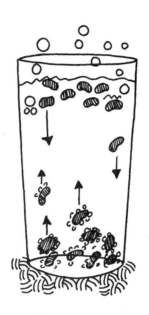

Engage Activity

Have a clear container of water. Have a variety of items—some that will sink, some that will float. Have students predict what each item will do before you put it in the water. Review why things float (they are lighter than water) or sink (they are heavier than water).

Experimenting/Observing

Have students fill their plastic glasses with the soda to within 1" (2.54 cm) of the top. Have them observe what they see happening. Add 10-15 raisins or popcorn kernels to the soda. Let them closely observe what happens within the glass. Allow plenty of time for observation.

Thinking

What are the bubbles in the soda? Are they heavier than or lighter than the soda? What happened to the raisins (or popcorn) when they were first put into the glass? What did you see gathering around the raisins (or popcorn) at the bottom of the glass? When do the raisins (or popcorn) begin to float to the top? Why do they again sink to the bottom? How long will this floating and sinking go on?

Science Notes

If you use raisins in this activity, the entire experiment can be consumed after you are finished! The raisin or popcorn kernel sinks because it is heavier than the soda it displaces. It floats when the carbon dioxide attaches to it and thus the total of the raisin plus carbon dioxide weighs less than the soda it displaces.

Explanation

The raisins (or popcorn) sink because they are heavier than (more dense than) the soda. When they reach the bottom, the carbon dioxide bubbles from the soda cling to the raisin (or popcorn) until there are enough to make it lighter than the soda. It then floats to the top. There the CO_2 bubbles burst into the air and the raisin (or popcorn) again becomes heavier than the soda and sinks. There is only so much CO_2 in the soda, and when it is all released the raisins will stay at the bottom.

Extension

You can quantify this activity by timing the process for several raisins and reaching an average amount of time at the beginning. Compare this with the rate as the amount of carbon dioxide diminishes.

82. Magnetic Attractions

Outcome
Students will experience the magnetic attraction between magnets and materials that are affected by magnetism.

Materials
- magnet for each student
- materials for testing (examples: thumbtack, screw, paper clip, metal spoon, plastic spoon, keys, coins, squares of aluminum foil, pencil, crayon)
- magnetic toy

Engage Activity
Display one of the novelty items that uses a series of magnetized components that can be rearranged in different shapes. Let students manipulate the magnets in this toy.

Experimenting/Observing
Let students manipulate the magnet and materials you have provided until they have a clear understanding of which items are subject to magnetic attraction.

Thinking
What does it feel like when something is attracted to the magnet? What are the things made of that are attracted to the magnet? Are all metals attracted to the magnet? Can you predict what will be attracted to a magnet and what will not be attracted?

Explanation
Magnetic attraction is a pull between objects. Magnets are attracted to certain metals. The most common are iron, cobalt, nickel and steel.

Science Notes
Electromagnetism is one of the guiding forces in our universe. Magnetic materials have molecules that are bi-polar domains. That means that they have a north end and a south end within the molecule. A magnet is very organized so that all north ends face the same way. When the magnet is close to a substance that has magnetic molecules (domains), there is attraction between north and south poles of the magnet and south and north poles of the magnetic substance. That attraction is felt as "pull" between the magnet and the magnetic substance.

83. Red Cabbage Juice Detective

Outcome
Students will learn how to test common substances to see if they are acid, base or neutral.

Materials
- red cabbage juice (Blend chopped outer leaves with warm water. Strain and keep clear juice refrigerated until ready to use.)
- materials for testing (Assign a number to each substance and label testing materials with number only.)
  acid materials: vinegar, lemon juice, soda, crushed vitamin C
  base materials: baking soda, shampoo, dishwashing detergent
      neutral materials: water, shaved Ivory® soap bar
- small, clear plastic containers for student testing
- plastic spoons, wooden stir sticks, eyedroppers

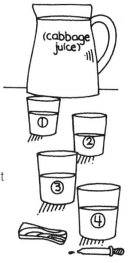

Engage Activity
Display items that scientists might use to identify a mysterious substance (microscope, magnifying lens, binoculars, scalpel, etc.). Discuss how students will be using red cabbage juice to help determine whether a mystery substance is an acid or a base. Acids are sour-tasting and have strong smells. Bases taste bitter and feel slippery to the touch. Neutral substances are an equal mix of acid and base. Strong acids and strong bases can be harmful, so NEVER taste anything until you know what it is and that it is safe to do so.

Experimenting/Observing
Put mystery substance in clear plastic container, add cabbage juice to cover then stir. Record color and number. Do this until all substances have been tested. Encourage repeats for accuracy and confirmation of data.

Thinking
Did anything stay the same color as the cabbage juice? What colors did you see in your mystery substances? What do you think the colors mean? How could this test help you identify mystery substances?

Explanation
Cabbage juice is a natural indicator of acids and bases. It will always change color when added to substances unless that substance is a weak acid. Colors seen will cover the color spectrum—orange, red, pink, purple, blue, green and yellow.* The color indicates whether the mystery substance is an acid or a base and how strong that acid or base is. Indicators can quickly narrow the possibilities of what a substance might be. (*See next page.)

Extension
The next activities are all extensions of this activity. You may want to incorporate them into this base activity for the older classroom. Third-graders handle the pH scale with surprising sophistication.

Science Notes
The most often asked question will be "can we pour them all together?" They can! Theoretically an acid and a base should yield water and a salt. Acids and bases are rated on a pH scale. The scale ranges from 1 to 14. Neutral is 7, strong acids are 1 and strong bases are 14. The pH of a substance is one accurate way of identifying it.

1 —6—7—8—— 14

strong acid   weak acid   neutral   weak base   strong base

84. The pH Scale

Outcome

Students will see how the red cabbage juice indicator tests are related to the pH scale of acids and bases.

Materials

- pH scale for Red Cabbage Juice Indicator poster, on chalkboard or copied for each student
- materials for "Red Cabbage Juice Detective" (page 83) plus any others you want tested

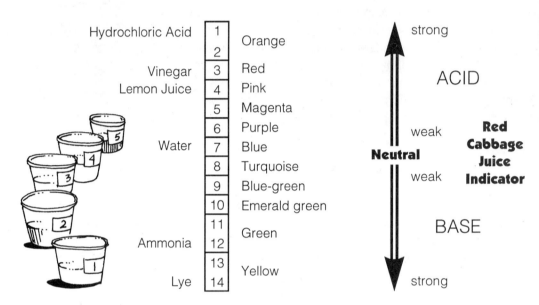

Hydrochloric Acid	1	Orange
	2	
Vinegar	3	Red
Lemon Juice	4	Pink
	5	Magenta
	6	Purple
Water	7	Blue
	8	Turquoise
	9	Blue-green
	10	Emerald green
	11	Green
Ammonia	12	
	13	Yellow
Lye	14	

strong
ACID
weak
Red Cabbage Juice Indicator
Neutral
weak
BASE
strong

Experimenting/Observing

Test substances. Record substance name, color change and pH number. Arrange tested materials from the strongest acid on the left to the strongest base on the right. Neutral substances will be in the middle.

Thinking

What does the pH scale tell you about a substance? Why must you record the substance and its color change?

Explanation

The pH scale gives us information about substances that are acids or bases, whether they are strong or weak. A substance will always have the same pH number so you can help identify an unknown with that information. Once you have added the cabbage juice, the substance no longer looks the same so you must keep careful records to keep track of what you have learned about a substance. Scientists always keep careful records of the data from their experiments.

Extension

You can spend some time looking into the kinds of things that are acids (food) and what are bases (cleaners). You may want to test substances until you have the whole pH spectrum.

Science Notes

pH refers to the power of hydrogen. Most acids will have hydrogen in their formula by itself (example: Hydrochloric Acid, HCl). Bases have their hydrogen tied up with oxygen (example: Lye, NaOH). Neutral substances have both hydrogen and hydrogen with oxygen (example: water H$_2$O or HOH).

85. Take-Home Test

Outcome
Students will prepare red cabbage juice indicator strips to take home to test household substances with parental supervision.

Materials
- red cabbage juice (see "Red Cabbage Juice Detective" on page 83 for directions)
- coffee filters (white)
- rulers
- scissors
- wax paper
- envelopes

strips

Immerse in cabbage juice...

Let dry...

Engage Activity
The "Red Cabbage Juice Detective" activity (page 83) should precede this activity. Talk about how students will be making detective kits to take home. Make a list of things they could test at home (shampoo, dish soap, soda pop, gelatin). Show them how to crush solids and mix with some water for testing with a strip.

Experimenting/Observing
Cut coffee filters into strips 3" x 1½" (7.62 x 3.79 cm). Immerse strips in cabbage juice. Remove and place strips on wax paper to dry. Put into envelopes to take home. Ask children to keep track of what they test at home by writing the substance tested on the strip. Parents can assist with this. Compare strips and experiences when brought back to classroom.

Take them home...

Thinking
Why did you use paper from coffee filters to make the strips? Were there a lot of acids and bases in your home?

Explanation
Coffee filters are made of very absorbent paper that will soak up a lot of cabbage juice. The strips have to have enough cabbage juice in them to indicate acid or base. There should be many acids and bases in your home. Foods tend to be acids; cleaners tend to be bases.

Extension
Have students test their saliva!

Science Notes
You will be making a litmus paper substitute that will give more information about the strength of an acid or a base. Hydrangeas are a garden flower that act as an indicator of soil acidity or alkalinity (baseness). Blue flowers for acid soil, pink for alkaline.

86. Secret Messages

Outcome
Students will use an acid/base indicator to write a message that then fades away. It can be brought back by adding a base.

Materials
- indicator paint (crush a phenolphthalein tablet [Exlax®] mix with 50 ml of water and 50 ml of ethyl alcohol—not rubbing alcohol)
- watercolor paper (rinsed and dried)
- paintbrushes
- needed at home: glass cleaner spray

Engage Activity
Prepare a sample message beforehand to surprise your students. Ask them what they see (nothing). Spray with glass cleaner to reveal message. Talk about how indicators tell us if there is an acid or base on the paper. You will be painting with an indicator and add the base by spraying with glass cleaner.

Experimenting/Observing
Have students write a message to parents. It must be simple as it will be applied with paintbrush. Have them put a border and any other picture/decorations they want on their message. Dry. Take home and have parents spray with glass cleaner to reveal message.

Thinking
What happened to your message when it dried? What happened to it when you sprayed it with a base (the glass cleaner)? How could you get the message to disappear?

Explanation
When your message dries you can no longer see the indicator that you painted on it so it is just a blank piece of paper again. When you spray the paper with a base, the indicator turns pink. You could make the pink disappear again by spraying with an acid like vinegar.

Extension
You could send secret messages to another class in school. Try painting messages with different acids and bases (lemon juice, liquid detergent, etc.) and spraying with cabbage juice.

Science Notes
Invisible inks have been a source of fun and intrigue for years. This is a fun activity to culminate your look into acids and bases.

87. How Strong Is Air?

Outcome
Students will see effects of air pressure by collapsing a plastic soda bottle.

Materials
- empty liter soda bottles with lids
- ice cubes
- sink with hot and cold water taps
- items for display (see below)

Engage Activity
Have on display an inflated bicycle tire, blown up balloons and an electric fan with streamers tied to the front grill. Discuss what role air plays in all these things. Take a vote to see whether air is strong enough to collapse a liter soda bottle.

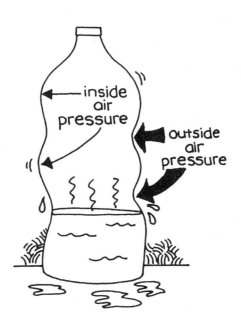

Experimenting/Observing
Fill sink with cold water and ice cubes. Have students fill their soda bottles about one-third full of hot water. Count to twenty. Put lid on bottle. Roll bottle in icy water for several minutes. Stand upright. Observe what happens to the bottle.

Thinking
Did the cold water crush your bottle? What did the cold water do to the temperature in your bottle? What was the only thing touching the outside of your bottle when you stood it upright? Which air was stronger, the cool air outside the bottle or the warm air inside the bottle?

Explanation
The cold water cooled the air inside your bottle. When warm air is cooled, it takes up less room. There was then room for more air in your bottle. The outside air tried to fill up that room and ended up pushing in the sides of the bottle. Air strength is called air pressure. Cold temperatures have high air pressure (strength); warm temperatures have low air pressure (strength).

Extension
You can do this with tin or aluminum cans that have screw-on lids for great sound effects. It sort of creaks at first and then goes pop, bang, screech as it squishes up. However, you usually can't get the can back to the original shape and reuse it.

Science Notes
Air is made of gas molecules. They have mass just as liquids and solids do. When gas molecules are heated, the added energy allows the molecules to move further apart, thus lowering air pressure. When air is cooled, there is a loss of energy and loss of movement. This makes the closely packed molecules have more pressure. An increase in elevation lowers air pressure as does movement of air (the basis of flight).

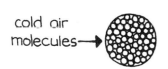

cold air molecules→

warm air molecules

88. Layers of Liquid

Outcome
Students will observe liquids of different densities floating and sinking in one another.

Materials
- light Karo® syrup
- salad oil
- water (colored blue)
- tall, plastic glasses
- plastic spoon

Engage Activity
Make a density detector. Attach a clay ball around the end of a straw. Have students watch as you place it in each liquid sample. Ask for guesses about what the density detector is telling you about these substances.

Experimenting/Observing
Have students pour the Karo® syrup into the bottom third of their glass. (Pour over back of spoon for less mess.) Pour another third full with salad oil. Fill glass almost full with water.

Thinking
Which liquid was on the bottom? Why?
Which liquid was in the middle? Why?
Which liquid was on top? Why?

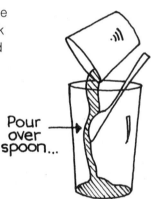

Pour over spoon...

Explanation
Liquids have different densities. The same amount of different liquids weigh more or less than each other. Karo® syrup is the most dense liquid, so it is on the bottom. Oil is the least dense, so it is on top. Water is more dense than oil but less dense than Karo®. Liquids can float in liquids just like solids can float in liquids; gases can float in gases or gases float in liquid.

Extension
The next activity will add solid objects to the glass for comparing densities of liquids and solids.

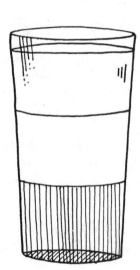

Science Notes
The concept of density is more easily comprehended with an example than with words. Density refers to how heavy something is for its size. Liquid densities are fun to experiment with.

89. Layers of Density

Outcome
Students will observe solid objects floating in one liquid and sinking in others according to solid densities and liquid densities.

Materials
- "layer of liquid": glass of Karo® syrup, water and salad oil
- items to float or sink: paper clips, macaroni, wood pieces, nuts and bolts, clay balls, apple slices—anything you and your students can think of and will fit into the glass

Engage Activity
"Layers of Liquid" (page 88) activity should precede this.

Experimenting/Observing
Carefully place objects in the glass.

Thinking
Do you have things that are floating on the water? On the oil? On the Karo® syrup? Can you predict what something will do before you put it in the glass? What happens to objects that are less dense than water but more dense than oil? What happens to objects that are more dense than water but less dense than Karo® syrup?

Explanation
The objects float or sink according to their density. If they are more dense than oil, water and Karo® syrup, they will sink to the bottom. If they are more dense than oil and water, but less dense than Karo® syrup, they will float in the Karo®. If they are more dense than oil but less dense than water, they will float in water. If they are less dense than oil, they will float in the oil.

Extension
Provide students with food coloring and a plastic spoon. Have them put several drops of food coloring into the glass. The drops will remain drops and not mix with the oil. Have them push the drops into the water. The drops will then mix with the water.

Science Notes
*This is a further look at densities. The extension activity shows that liquids don't always mix. We find that many things are soluble (will mix) in water. In this instance, the food coloring is **not** soluble in oil and is less dense than water. When pushed into the water, the food coloring dissolves into the water.*

90. Tricky Inertia

Outcome
Students will learn to do a demonstration that depends on inertia. They will understand why this demonstration works.

Materials
For each student:
- coffee mug
- small box (match, paper clip, etc.)
- 4" x 6" (10.16 x 15.24 cm) index card
- 2" (5.08 cm) Styrofoam™ ball

Engage Activity
Have students pretend they are in a car. Describe the car speeding away from a stop sign. Have them demonstrate what will be happening to their bodies (thrown against the back of the seat). Explain that their head was trying to stay where it had been because of *inertia*. This means that a thing not in motion will stay still until some force makes it move (Newton's First Law of Motion—a body at rest tends to remain at rest unless acted upon by an outside force.)

Experimenting/Observing
Fold up 1" (2.54 cm) at the back of the index card. Put on mug top. Stand box on its edge on top of card. Balance ball on top of box. Quickly pull card away from mug so that the folded edge catches the box. Practice until you feel comfortable enough to do it at home.

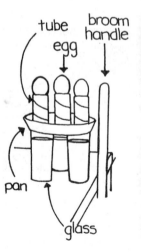

Thinking
What happens to the ball in your experiment? What happens to the box? What force acts on the box? Is there any force acting on the ball to make it move to the side? What force acts upon it to make it fall into the mug? Can you repeat this experiment at home? Can you explain why it happened?

Explanation
When you moved the index card the folded portion was a force that pulled the box off to the side. The box went into motion because of the outside force of the index card. The ball did not have any outside force working on it but gravity. The force of gravity pulled it into the mug. If you did this demonstration in space, the ball would remain where it is because there would be NO force working on it to make it move.

Extension
Plan a science show for another class or parents that involves similar demonstrations. Try the following with the whole class helping in the preparation: Place three hard-boiled eggs in the top of three cardboard toilet paper tubes. Put these on top of a metal pie plate. Put the plate on top of tall, plastic glasses three-fourths full of water, positioned under the eggs. Place next to the edge of a desktop. Using a stiff broom that is positioned flush with the bottom of the desk, pull the broom handle back and quickly let go. Eggs SHOULD land in the water. Restack and do again until everyone can do it. Isn't science fun?

Science Notes
Inertia is the resistance objects have to a change in movement. The greater the mass of an object, the greater its inertia. This means that heavy objects need a greater force to stop or to start their movement than lightweight objects. The mighty tugboat is needed to start an ocean liner in movement through the water. Comparing the brake systems of a bus and a bicycle show that a greater force is needed to stop the heavier bus. Defensive linemen on a football team have great mass so that the inertia of their forward move-ment is hard for the opposing team to stop!

91. Friction Works for You

Outcome
Students will examine the concept of friction and how their everyday lives are affected by it.

Materials
For the classroom:
- door handle
- liquid dish or hand soap
- items for display (see below)
- water
- towels

Engage Activity
Display bicycle tire, hiking boot, rubber-backed place mat, anything that has a surface that stops something from sliding. Ask students what all these things have in common. Discuss each item and how it uses friction to help you.

Experimenting/Observing
Have students examine the soles of their shoes. Compare and contrast soles among the class members. See if they can decide whose shoes will stop the fastest. Have students briskly rub their hands together. Ask how their hands feel after they have done this. Explain that when friction is at work there is heat produced. Have each student use the friction between his hand and a door handle to twist the handle. Have each student wet her hands with soap and water and try to twist the handle again. Have each student try to write his name on a windowpane with a lead pencil.

Thinking
What would it be like to walk on shoes that had soles made of glass? Why do we have such fancy soles on our shoes? Why couldn't you open the door with soap and water on your hands? Compare this to a wet highway. Why couldn't you write your name on the window?

Explanation
The friction between the soles of your feet or your shoes help you remain in balance when you walk and to stop when you want to. The fancy soles on sports shoes make sure we will not slip and will stop when we want to. The soap and water interfered with the friction between your hand and the door handle. They slipped past one another so that you couldn't open the door. Icy or wet highways interfere with friction between a tire and the road and can result in cars that are out of control. You could not write your name on the window because there was not enough friction between the glass and the lead of your pencil to rub some of the lead off.

Extension
Explore air friction on cars and bike rides. What designs have resulted from trying to cut down on this friction?

Science Notes
Friction on Earth means never having a perpetual motion machine! There is always friction with air molecules.

92. Multiplying with Mirrors

Outcome
Students will observe how mirrors reflect light from images and how multiple images can be seen.

Materials
For each student or group of students:
- 2 small mirrors
- short pencil or crayon
- small object such as a marble

Engage Activity
Take students into one of the school lavatories with big mirrors. Have students raise their right hands and ask what hand their reflection is holding up. Make sure students understand that mirrors reflect things the wrong way around. This is called a mirror image. Explain that *reflections* occur when light from an object is bounced back off a shiny surface.

Experimenting/Observing
Put your mirrors together face to face. Open one side so that you can put your small object in between them. As you open and close the mirrors, count how many reflections of your object you can see. Place your pencil with the point touching one mirror, the end touching the other. Count the number of sides in the shape you have made. Open and close the mirrors to make other shapes with different numbers of sides. Place the two mirrors so that they face each other. Put your object in between them. Look in the mirrors. Try to count how may reflections of the object you can see now.

Thinking
What was the lowest number of objects that you could see? What was the highest number? What did the mirrors do with each reflection that came to its surface? Did you see more reflections when the mirrors were closer together? Why do you think that you saw so many reflections when the mirrors were facing each other?

Explanation
The lowest number of objects you could see was three. Each mirror reflected only one image. As you moved the mirrors closer together they reflected more and more images. When the mirrors were face to face, they reflected many images because the images were reflected back and forth, back and forth between the mirrors.

Extension
Write secret codes. Write with wooden craft stick on paper with upside-down carbon paper underneath. Mirror writing will be on the back of the paper.

Science Notes
Objects reflect at the angle they strike the mirror. This makes it possible to manipulate numbers of images.

93. Fast Air vs. Slow Air

Outcome

Students will learn that fast-flowing air creates low air pressure. They will create low-pressure areas around objects to obtain "lift" and correlate this to the lift and flight of nonjet airplanes.

Materials

For each student or group of students:
- 10" (25.4 cm) length of adding machine tape or similar cut paper strip
- thread
- Scotch™ tape
- 2 Ping-Pong™ balls
- scissors
- ruler

Engage Activity

Display nonjet model airplanes. Have students determine what part of the plane is essential for it to fly.

Experimenting/Observing

Tape a long piece of thread to each Ping-Pong™ ball. Tape the other ends of the threads 3" (7.62 cm) apart on a door frame or other place where balls can hang freely. When balls are completely still, blow as hard as you can in between them. Observe what happens. Take paper strip and place on your lower lip. Blow strongly on the top side of the paper strip. Observe what happens. Fold and crease paper strip crosswise. Fold back the other way and tape so that one end is shorter than another. Place your wing shape strip against your lower lip so that the curved side is up. Blow along the curved side. Observe what happens.

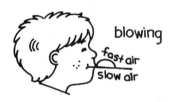

Thinking

What happened when you blew between the Ping-Pong™ balls? Was the fast-moving air as strong as the air on the outside edges of the Ping-Pong™ balls? What happened when you blew on the strip of paper? Why did the paper come up? Was the fast-moving air weaker than the air below the strip? What happened when you blew on the wing shape? Did the wing-shaped paper rise more quickly that the straight piece of paper? Why are wings of airplanes shaped the way they are?

Explanation

The strength of air is called *air pressure*. Moving air has less air pressure than air that is not moving. When you blew between the Ping-Pong™ balls or on the top of the paper you made that air have less pressure (less strength) than the air on the other side of the objects. The stronger air pressure then pushed the objects. The Ping-Pong™ balls were pushed together. The strip of paper was pushed up. When air pressure pushes something up it is called *lift*. Your wing shape helped increase the air pressure below the wing and so it moved up very quickly.

Science Notes

This is a first look at Bernoulli's principle that explains how fast moving air (or fluids) has less pressure (strength) than slower moving air (or fluid). This principle led to the understanding of flight and the field of aerodynamics.

94. How to Bend the Light

Outcome
Students will see that light rays bend when traveling through water.

Materials
For each group of students:
- small bowl (cannot be translucent)
- plastic drinking glass with water
- penny

Engage Activity
Make a light ray bender box and demonstrate for students. To make box: Put a thin slit in one end of a shoe box. Fill a square glass jar with water and set in middle of box. Shine flashlight through slit and into jar.

Experimenting/Observing
Place penny in bottom of bowl. Back away from bowl until you can no longer see the penny. Have another student begin to fill bowl with water. Observe what seems to happen to the penny while this is done. Empty bowl of water. Redo experiment for each student in your group.

Thinking
What could you see after a small amount of water was placed in the bowl? What did you observe as the bowl was filled with water? Why were you able to see the penny once water was added to the bowl?

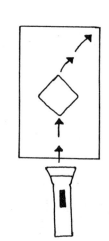

Explanation
As the bowl was filled with water, more and more of the penny became visible to you. Since the penny did not move and you did not move, it had to be the light rays coming from the penny that moved. When the light reflected by the penny moved through the water and then into the air, it was bent. This bending moved the light rays so that they could be seen by you.

Extension
Using tubs of water, observe how light rays make submerged objects appear closer to the surface than they really are.

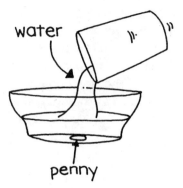

water

penny

Science Notes
Light moves through different substances at different speeds. The slowing down and speeding up that occurs when it changes from one material to another results in the bending of light rays. Any bending of light is called "refraction." The light rays coming from the penny are refracted (bent) when they leave the water and enter the air. They are bent toward the eye of the observer, and thus the penny seems to rise from the bowl. The angle of refraction can be controlled and used for various purposes. Lenses refract light to enable observers to see more clearly (glasses) or to see things magnified (microscopes).

95. Traveling Light Rays

Outcome
Students will see light rays travel in a straight line.

Materials
For each student or group of students:
- 4" x 6" (10.16 x 15.24 cm) index cards (at least three)
- ruler
- hole punch
- flashlight

Engage Activity
Turn out lights and use a flashlight to point out various familiar objects in the classroom, including individual students. Discuss how light must travel for you to be able to shine the flashlight so that certain things are lit up and not the rest of the room.

Experimenting/Observing
Fold index cards in half. Punch holes in all cards but one. Punch holes in center of card while pushing card completely into the punch. Set cards in a row so that the card without a hole is the furthest from you. Aim flashlight through the hole in the first card, line up the other cards so that light passes through those holes all the way to the furthest card. Stick your finger into the light beam. Observe what happens. Move one of the cards with a hole. Observe what happens.

Thinking
What happens to the light when all the holes are lined up? Are any of the cards except the first one completely lit up from the flashlight beam? What happens when you put a finger in the beam of light or move one of the cards?

Explanation
Light travels in a straight line from its source (the flashlight). The light will travel to the back card if all the holes are lined up in a straight line. The only light that hits each card after the first one is a tiny beam going in a straight line. Those light rays that aren't in a straight line through the hole in the card are blocked. You can block the light rays with your finger or by moving a card.

Extension
Look at different light sources: Household light bulb, flashlight, spotlight, etc. See if students can determine where the light will travel from these sources.

Science Notes
Although it seems that light can fill up all the spaces when coming from the sun or a light bulb, a single light ray can only travel in a straight line. This is why we have shadows formed in any kind of light. Flashlights limit light to a stream directly in front of it, the holes limit the light rays even more. Light rays are bent in traveling through different materials.

96. You Light Up My Bulb

Outcome
Students will understand that current electricity flows in a circle.

Materials
For each student or group of students:
- 1.5-volt bulb and bulb holder
- 1.5-volt battery
- 2 strands of coated electrical wire, 6" (15.24 cm) long, ends stripped

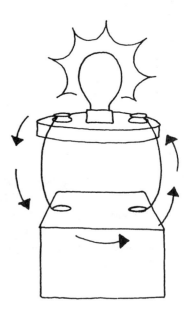

Engage Activity
Display some battery-operated toys and household objects without their batteries. Have students determine what is missing. Insert batteries and operate devices.

Experimenting/Observing
Put one wire around one end of the battery and one post of the bulb holder. Repeat with other wire around other end of battery and other post of bulb holder. Observe and describe what you see happen and when it happens. Unhook one wire and observe what happens. For the younger student, set up everything in advance so that all they will do is unhook and hook one wire.

Thinking
What provides the electricity for the bulb to light up? How does the electricity get to the bulb? What will happen if one wire is not attached to the power source? What will happen if one wire is not attached to the bulb holder? What path has the electricity taken in your experiments?

Explanation
The battery provided the electricity for the bulb to light up. The materials inside the battery have chemicals that conduct electricity. Wires carry electricity to and from the bulb. If one wire is not attached, the electricity cannot flow. Electricity must travel in a circle to deliver electricity to the bulb.

Extension
Gently break a burned-out light bulb. Show students the filament that gives off light and heat as electricity flows through it. The filament is made of tungsten.

Science Notes
Current electricity moves in a path unlike static electricity where charges stay still. Current electricity is carried in wires by the flow of charged electrons along the wire. When that flow is interrupted, electrical energy is no longer available to use. Batteries use a chemical reaction to produce the moving electrons. They are small, portable and have many uses. Batteries have different strengths known as volts. More volts, more electrons in motion. Household electricity is produced at a central location and carried by wires from that point. Household electricity is produced from chemical reactions (burning coal) or conversion of kinetic energy (hydroelectric dams). Storms can interrupt the flow of household electricity.

97. What Things Will Carry Electricity?

Outcome
Students will be able to see what things will carry an electrical current and what things will not carry and electrical current.

Materials
For each student or group of students:
- 1.5-volt bulb and bulb holder
- 1.5-volt battery
- 3 strands of coated electrical wire, 6" (15.24 cm) long, ends stripped
- materials to test: lemon wedges, brass paper fasteners, paper clips, water in a paper cup, plastic pen, crayon, etc.

Engage Activity
Discuss electrical safety in the bathroom. Ask students why we must be careful around electricity and water.

Experimenting/Observing
Put one wire around one end of the battery and attach it to one post of the bulb holder. Put the next wire around the other end of the battery. Put the last wire around the other post of the bulb holder. Holding the wire by the coated part, touch the two bare wires together and observe what happens. Place the materials to test on a table. Test samples to see if they carry electricity by sticking the two bare wires into samples. Always be sure to handle the wire by the coating. For the younger student, set up everything in advance so that all they'll have to do is test the different objects.

Thinking
How did you know that one of your test items could carry an electrical current? Can you describe the path of electricity in each test? What happened when the electricity could not travel in a circle?

Explanation
When an item was able to carry an electrical current, the electricity flowed through it and the light bulb would light up. When an item could not carry electricity, the circle was broken and the bulb did not light up.

Extension
Have students add items from the classroom to test. The low voltage insures that everyone is safe. Determine which items are the best conductors of electricity and which are not. The amount of light coming from the bulb is your indicator.

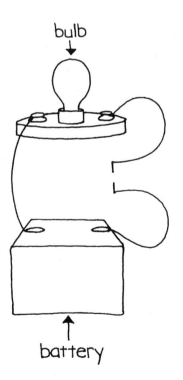

bulb

battery

Science Notes
Because you have set up a low-voltage system, this is an appropriate time for students to learn just what is safe and what is not safe in their own environments. Materials that act as good conductors for electrical currents have more electrons that are free to carry the electricity through the materials. Materials that do not carry electricity are called "insulators." Their electrons are not free to move about as are the electrons in a conductor. Metals are almost always good conductors because of their atomic structure. Students should be warned that the voltage from car batteries and from household electrical outlets are so high they can cause great harm.

98. Charged-Up Balloons

Outcome
By experimenting with static electricity in balloons, students will understand the concepts of attraction and repulsion associated with negative and positive electrical charges.

Materials
For each student of group of students:
- 2 inflated balloons
- 20 construction paper dots made with hole punch
- felt-tip marker
- fabric swatches of silk and wool

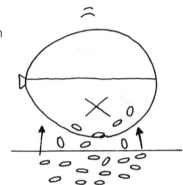

Engage Activity
Rub a balloon on your hair and place it on the wall. Charge other balloons with silk and wool and do the same. Ask students if they have explanations for what they are seeing.

Experimenting/Observing
Spread out the paper dots on your desk. Draw a line with the marker that divides your balloons in half. Mark one half of each balloon with an X. Rub the X half of the balloon vigorously in your hair. Put the half without the X close to the dots. Observe. Rub both balloon halves with the X in your hair. Put the balloons on your desk and observe what happens when you put the two X sides close together.

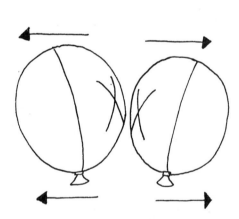

Thinking
What happened to the dots when you put the uncharged side of the balloon close to them? What happened when you put the charged side next to them? Do you know the name of the force that made the dots jump up? What happened when you put the X sides of the two balloons close together? Why do you think this happened?

Explanation
Static electricity results when materials have a charge. You gave the balloon a negative charge by rubbing it. The dots had a positive charge. "Unlike" charges are attracted to one another. "Like" charges repel (push away from) one another. The positive-charged dots were attracted to the negative-charged balloon. When you put the charged parts of the two balloons close together, they repelled one another.

Extension
Have students move balloons using repelling forces.

Science Notes
When some things are rubbed together, electrons are rubbed off leaving one material with a positive charge and the other with a negative charge. The negative charges of the balloon repelled the negative charges of the dots and they moved to the underside of the dots. This leaves a positive side which leaps to the balloon. Matter normally has no charge, but static electricity can easily be created. Electrical storms are but a large display of static electricity caused by rubbing raindrops.

99. Jumping to the Music

Outcome
Students will see direct evidence that sounds produce vibrations.

Materials
For each student or group of students:
- small, round plastic container (margarine tub, etc.)
- rubber bands that will go around the container
- gallon-sized plastic bags
- ¼ teaspoon (1.25 ml) rice
- ¼ teaspoon (1.25 ml) sugar
- portable radio with speakers (can be shared)
- tuning fork

Engage Activity
Use tuning forks to demonstrate vibrations produced by sound. Have students feel their throats and then their lips while they make low noises. Have them quickly flap their hands to show motion of vibration. Survey students to make sure everyone understands the motion that is vibration.

Experimenting/Observing
Place plastic bag over top of container. Stretch the rubber bands around the bowl to keep the bag in place. Make sure the plastic is pulled tight like a drum across the top. Put rice on top of drum and place in front of speaker while music is playing loudly. Observe what happens to the rice. Take off the rice and put on the sugar. Again, put in front of speaker. Observe what happens to the sugar.

Thinking
What do you see happening to the rice and the sugar when it is by the speakers? What has made it act this way? Can you see what happens when there is no sound coming from the speaker? If not, observe again.

Explanation
The rice and the sugar begin to dance in time to the music coming from the speaker. Sound is carried by vibrating air. That air made the plastic of your drum vibrate, too. When that happened, your rice and sugar began to move up and down. When there was no sound, there was no movement of the rice or sugar.

Extension
Try to pinpoint which notes make the rice and sugar move the most. Vary the volume of the radio as students observe the motion of the sugar and rice.

Science Notes
Yes, a tree falling in a forest makes a sound. Sound is a form of energy produced by vibrations. When something begins to vibrate, it makes the air vibrate also. The energy is then carried to our ears by vibrating air molecules. Eventually the vibration is transferred to our eardrums, and the complex mechanism of translating vibration to recognized sound begins.

100. A Loud Sound Box

Outcome
Students will make an amplifier and experience how sound vibrations can be increased.

Materials
For each student or group of students:
- empty milk carton or carry-out food carton
- 1' (.30 m) string
- crayon stub or pencil stub
- pencil with point
- paper cup with water
- empty wastebasket (metal is best)
- vinegar
- glass

Engage Activity
Talk into an empty wastebasket. Have students compare the sound to your normal voice. Dampen clean forefinger with vinegar. Rub around rim of a glass until you produce a loud sound. Ask students to guess what is producing the sound (the vibrations your finger begins) and why it is so loud (all the material in the glass vibrates).

Experimenting/Observing
Wet the string and hold it firmly with one hand. Use your thumb and forefinger of the other hand and quickly pull the string taut. Observe any sound. Poke a hole in the bottom of the carton. Put string though the hole from outside to inside. Tie the end of the string around the pencil or crayon stub so that the string is secure. Wet string again, hold carton with one hand and pull down on the string with your thumb and forefinger. Observe sound.

Science Notes
Amplification depends on forcing another surface area to vibrate. This is the concept behind speakers for radio and television. The incoming sound energy forces the speakers to vibrate at the same frequencies over a large area, hence, a louder sound is produced. Dry string will not vibrate enough to produce satisfactory quality sound. The water and material in the string together vibrate to make the squeak.

Thinking
What sound was produced by the wet string before you put it in the carton? How was the sound from the wet string different when it was attached to the carton? What was vibrating to make noise when the string was by itself? What else began to vibrate when you attached the string to the carton?

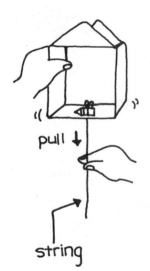

Explanation
The wet string produced a small squeaky sound by itself. When it was attached to the carton, the sound was amplified to a loud squeak. The carton amplified the sound because the string vibrations were transferred to the carton and made the material in the carton vibrate. The larger the surface area that vibrates, the louder the sound.

Extension
Use an empty tin can for a different sound. Place the base of a vibrating tuning fork on your desk.

Safety Tips for Using Open Flame in the Classroom

Do not use open flame activities in your classroom if it is against school regulations.

Open flame activities are recommended as DEMONSTRATION ONLY with young children.

Make sure the fire extinguisher in your classroom is in working order and that you are comfortable in its operation.

Bring a thick wool blanket to class to smother flames.

On each desk, place a very damp bath towel that can quickly be thrown over a flame. Make sure students know to do this.

Remember to treat burns with cool water and notify the nurse immediately. Remove hot wax quickly from skin.

Check that students have short-sleeved clothes on or have rolled up their sleeves.

Stress to students that most burns occur when they place their bare arm across the top of the flame. Science experimenting demands constant awareness of students and teachers.

Safety in Science

It is always a wise idea to begin your school year with a serious discussion about safety while doing science activities. Students should be encouraged to come up with their own safety rules. The following ideas should be added to that list if they are not already included:

- Follow directions carefully.
- Measure carefully.
- Treat equipment carefully.
- Report accidents to the teacher immediately.
- Clean up work areas after science time is over.
- Taste and smell only with permission.
- Stay alert while experimenting.
- Share ideas and results with classmates so that they can learn.
- Return equipment and materials to their proper place in the classroom.

If you are able to visit a laboratory setting, have your tour guides point out what safety measures they observe.

Suggested List of Basic Classroom Materials for Science Activities

The activities in this book require materials that can be easily obtained. Many will be used in several activities. This list is a starting point for equipping your classroom for science discovery.

- magnifying lenses (10X, plastic with swivel case)
- hand-held illuminating microscope (30X, plastic with snap case)
- paper towel and toilet paper cardboard tubes
- PVC tubing (purchase at hardware store)
- 1.5-volt bulb and bulb holder, 1.5-volt battery
- coated electrical wire, wire strippers
- strainers (can be homemade with screening and 1" x 1" [2.54 x 2.54 cm] lumber)
- lemon juice, baking soda, cornstarch, kosher salt, vinegar, light Karo® syrup, salad oil
- plastic margarine tubs with lids
- large tubs (dishwashing size)
- Ping-Pong™ balls, 2" (5.08 cm) Styrofoam™ balls
- tea light candles, regular candles
- measuring cups and spoons
- empty salad dressing bottles
- plastic spoons and knives
- modeling clay
- corks
- floating toys
- bar magnets
- compasses
- balances or scales
- empty plastic soda bottles
- paper cups
- food coloring
- eyedroppers
- plastic flashlights
- plastic drinking glasses
- coffee filters
- rocks, gravel, sand
- string
- thermometers
- iodine
- small mirrors
- balloons
- straws
- wooden craft sticks

Directions for Laminating Oversized Materials

Fold material to be laminated in half. Run through laminator. Slit open side opposite fold. Refold the opposite way. Run through laminator. Slit open side opposite fold.

First...

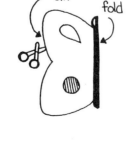

Then...

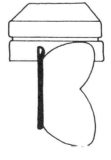

Next...

Last...

Award Badge Samples

These can be used for Family Science Night awards and at other times that call for rewarding good sciencing!

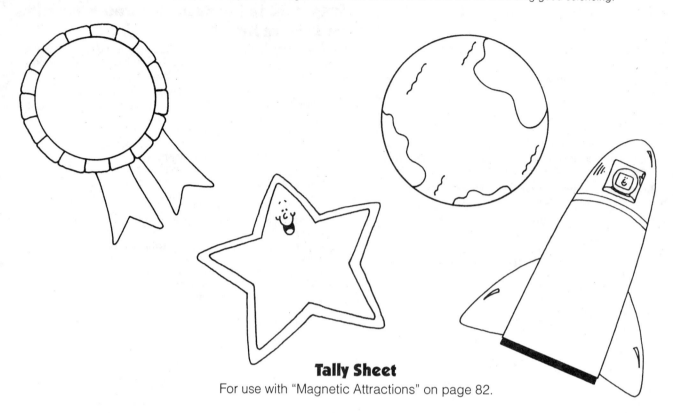

Tally Sheet

For use with "Magnetic Attractions" on page 82.

Material	Attracted ✔	Not Attracted ✔

Family Science Night Flyers

Family Science Night!
What Lives in Our Neighborhood?

Place _____

Day _____

Time _____

Please bring: _____

_____

_____

Other directions: _____

_____

_____

Family Science Night!
Family Feet

Place _____

Day _____

Time _____

Please bring: _____

_____

_____

Other directions: _____

_____

_____

Family Science Night!
Hiding in Plain Sight

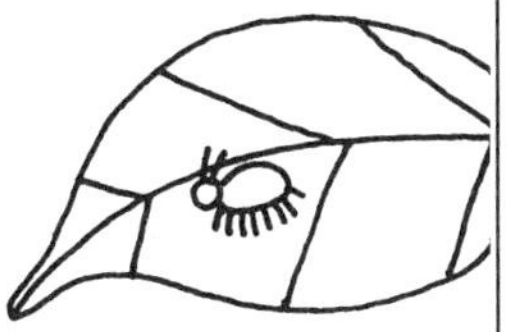

Place _____

Day _____

Time _____

Please bring: _____

_____

_____

Other directions: _____

_____

_____

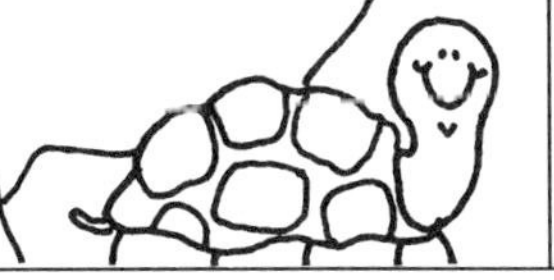

Family Science Night!
Recycle and Reuse

Place _____

Day _____

Time _____

Please bring: _____

_____

_____

Other directions: _____

_____

_____

What Lives in Our Neighborhood? Data Sheet

Family Members: _____

_____
_____
_____
_____

Day	Animal	Location

Clouds

For use with "Clouds That Tell the Weather" on page 45.

Paper Doll Outline

For use with "Paper Kids!" on page 16.